MW00861142

Return:
Daily Inspiration for the Days of Awe

Erica Brown

RETURN

Daily Inspiration for the Days of Awe

Maggid Books and OU Press

Return: Daily Inspiration for the Days of Awe

First edition, 2012
Second printing

Maggid Books
An imprint of Koren Publishers Jerusalem Ltd.

POB 8531, New Milford, CT 06776-8531, USA
& POB 4044, Jerusalem 91040, Israel
www.korenpub.com

OU Press
An imprint of the Orthodox Union

11 Broadway
New York, NY 10004
www.oupress.org

The publication of this book was made possible through the generous support of *Torah Education in Israel.*

ISBN 978 159 264 3639, *hardcover*

A CIP catalogue record for this title is available from the British Library.

Printed and bound in the United States

"'Come, let us reach an understanding,' says the Lord.
'Be your sins like crimson, they can turn snow-white;
Be they red as dyed wool, they can become like fleece.'"

(Isaiah 1:18)

To my students,
who constantly show me
the meaning of growth and change,
and make all darkness white and pure.

In Loving Memory of Our Parents

Joseph and Gwendolyn Straus
יוסף שמואל בן בנימין
גינגדל בת משה יעקב

Dedicated by
Moshael and Zahava Straus
Daniel and Joyce Straus

Contents

Foreword

OU Press is proud to join with Maggid Books in co-publishing Erica Brown's sensitive and searching exploration of the world of teshuva.

For many, Maimonides' classic, *The Laws of Repentance*, gives structure to the emotional, psychological, intellectual, and religious components of teshuva, and serves as a wellspring of understanding for teshuva. Dr. Brown includes selections from *The Laws of Repentance* in each chapter of this excellent book. In her Preface, she mentions the custom of studying one of the ten chapters of *The Laws of Repentance* on each day of *Asseret Yemei Teshuva*. Teshuva is a goal; it comes in stages, intermittently. Our daily study reflects this concept of teshuva as an incremental process. Rabbi Joseph Soloveitchik, the towering rabbinic authority of the twentieth century, notes this custom with approval in his *Al HaTeshuva*, and relates that his father, as well as his grandfather, the famed Rav Hayim of Brisk, studied one chapter of *The Laws of Repentance* on each day of *Asseret Yemei Teshuva*. Rabbi Soloveitchik speculates that the division of the work into ten chapters may well have been a deliberate allusion by Maimonides to the ten days of *Asseret Yemei Teshuva*.

Maimonides highlights the unique quality of *Asseret Yemei Teshuva*: "Even though any time is appropriate for teshuva and prayer, during the ten days between Rosh HaShana and Yom Kippur teshuva is more appropriate, and it is accepted immediately." In one of the most lyrical passages in all of halakhic literature, Maimonides describes the power of teshuva: "How wonderful teshuva is, that it brings one close to the Divine Presence. Teshuva brings close those who are far away. Only yesterday he was loathed by the Almighty, repulsive, distant, and despicable; and today he is beloved, pleasing, close, and dear.... How lofty and exalted is the power of teshuva. Only yesterday he was separated from the God of Israel, crying out to no avail, and today he cleaves to the Divine Presence, cries out, and is answered immediately." It is this magical transformative gift of teshuva which Dr. Brown so effectively helps us grasp.

Erica Brown has had an exceptional impact on the Jewish scene. With her rare ability to convey the wisdom of our sages to a contemporary audience, she has raised an awareness of Jewish learning that is striking. We are indebted to her for this book, in which she gives us the tools to navigate the process of teshuva during the time between Rosh HaShana and Yom Kippur, a time suffused with hope and promise.

We wish to thank Moshael and Zahava Straus and Daniel and Joyce Straus for their generous sponsorship of this book.

Menachem Genack
General Editor, OU Press

Preface

We are embarking on a quest into the self during the ten days between Rosh HaShana and Yom Kippur – the *Asseret Yemei Teshuva*. Difficult work lies ahead.

Believing the words of our prayers during this season – namely that repentance, prayer, and charity annul the evil decree – many people have the custom of intensifying their good works and charitable impulses during these ten days. It is customary to increase one's performance of mitzvot and study during this period. Some people are even more scrupulous in their *kashrut* observance. While cynics may think this is just hedging one's bets, we all recognize the importance of building up spiritual muscle with enhanced use during a period of judgment. Good habits breed better habits and have a spillover effect from one day to the next. Whatever we can do to stimulate greater piety, introspection, and goodness will help us in the coming year to be more loving, more pious, more thoughtful, and more kind.

The pages ahead contain food for thought (even when we're fasting) for each of these ten days. Each day offers an essay on a biblical or rabbinic theme related to self-improvement and presents "Life Homework," a behavioral charge to help us exercise that muscle practically.

Each chapter ends with text questions on three passages for study that span almost a thousand years of Jewish learning. The first comes from *The Laws of Repentance* written by Maimonides (1135–1204); the ten chapters in *The Laws of Repentance* inspired many people to study one chapter a day for these ten days. The second passage is from *The Path of the Just* by Rabbi Moshe Haim Luzzatto (1707–1746). The third source is *The Lights of Repentance,* written by Rabbi Abraham Isaac HaCohen Kook (1865–1935). The texts gathered in the study section and throughout embody thousands of years of thinking and dreaming about what it means to become a better person in Jewish tradition.

Many works of self-improvement cited in the pages that follow surfaced during the *Musar* movement, a nineteenth-century ethical/behavioral crusade that spread throughout Eastern Europe largely in response to the over-intellectualization of Judaism. Teshuva means return. *Musar* means turn. Both filter into Jewish writings to reflect a profound desire to fix that which is broken, repair relationships, and strengthen intimacy with God.

Teshuva, the belief and the mandate that we really can and must change, is one of the greatest gifts that Judaism gave the world. And it is one of the greatest gifts we can give ourselves, one that demands hard internal work because teshuva requires good decision-making. The poet Robert Browning once bemoaned the difficulty of making decisions: "Life's business being just the terrible choice." But choose we must: every word we say, every small gesture, every action is a decision that has a causal impact on the next decision. Every day, three times daily according to tradition, we pray for forgiveness, appealing to God as both parent and judge: "Forgive us, our Father, for we have sinned. Pardon us, our King, for we have transgressed, for You pardon and forgive. Blessed are You, Lord, the gracious One who repeatedly forgives." We repeatedly sin so we ask that God repeatedly forgive. We make a daily habit of asking for God's pardon. But at this time of the year, we ask that God give us the wisdom and strength to make good decisions so that our repeated pattern of moral weakness and apology will finally be broken.

The Hasidic master, Rabbi Simha Bunim of Pzhysha, once said, "On Rosh HaShana the world begins anew, and before it begins anew, it comes to a close. Just as before dying, all the powers of the body clutch hard at life, so a person at the turn of the year ought to clutch at life with all his strength and might."[1]

ACKNOWLEDGMENTS

My great thanks extend to the team at Maggid Books and OU Press: Matthew Miller, Gila Fine, Deena Glickman, Deena Nataf, Shoshana Rotem, Menachem Genack, Simon Posner, and everyone else who helped move this from an idea into a hard-copy reality. Thank you for being critical readers and supportive friends. As always, I am grateful to the institutions that have nurtured my work for many years, to my friends and colleagues at the Jewish Federation of Greater Washington, the Avi Chai Foundation, the Covenant Foundation, the Wexner Foundation, and the Mandel Center.

As always, my loving friends and family occupy the center of my appreciation. In the spirit of repentance, having a wonderful husband and children gives both reason and cause to work on myself to become a better person. That I constantly fall short is no reason to stop trying. And my thanks, of course, goes to the Ultimate Writer, who will inscribe us all in the book of life if we pray with intensity, love with expansiveness, and practice goodness with all of our strength. In the words of Yehuda Amichai,

> I want once more to be written
> in the book of life, to be written
> anew every day
> until the writing hand hurts.

Erica Brown
Summer 5772, 2012

Notes

1. As retold in Martin Buber, *Tales of the Hasidim: Later Masters* (New York: Schocken Books, 1977), 252.

NOTE ON TRANSLATION

Many Hebrew classics have been used in these pages. In rare instances, I have used my own translation or paraphrasing, and it will be noted. Otherwise, the biblical translations rely upon the Koren Bible and the Jewish Publication Society (1999 Masoretic edition). Prayer excerpts have been taken from the *Metsudah Machzor* for both Rosh HaShana (1983) and Yom Kippur (1985). The passages of Maimonides for the study sections at the end of each chapter come from *Mishneh Torah* (*The Book of Knowledge*), *The Laws of Repentance,* translated by Eliyahu Touger (New York: Moznaim Publishing Corp., 1990). *The Laws of Personality Development* was translated by Eliyahu Touger and Za'ev Abramson (New York: Moznaim Publishing Corp., 1989); *The Guide of the Perplexed* excerpts are by Shlomo Pines (Chicago: University of Chicago Press, 1963). *The Path of the Just* translations are by Shraga Silverstein (Jerusalem: Feldheim Publishers, 1980) and Yosef Leibler (Jerusalem: Feldheim Publishers, 2004), and *The Lights of Repentance* excerpts are by either Ben Zion Bokser in The Classics of Western Spirituality series (Mahwah, NJ: Paulist Press, 1978) or by Alter Metzger in the Yeshiva University Press volume (New York: 1978).

Translation is an art. It is also a frustration. Therefore, I tried not to rely upon only one version when I felt that another rendered an expression easier to understand in English. Critical editions are often even more obfuscating for the uninitiated reader. That being said, virtually no translation can encompass the beauty or clarity of the Hebrew in its original; translations are oblique at best and confounding at worst. In the spirit of the book, if the English obscures the meaning, I apologize.

Introduction

Teshuva as Recovery

"For the sin we committed before You by being stubborn."

Rabbi Jonah of Gerona (d. 1263) called repentance a sanctuary, a place to escape the intensity of sin. It is also the place to embrace the strength needed to fight our hardest inner battles and our stubborn resistance to change. By calling repentance a sanctuary, Rabbi Jonah in *Sha'arei Teshuva* (The Gates of Repentance) transformed an act into a space we can step into and know that we are home, and we are safe. We have returned to our essential selves, the people we like best. We are at one with forces that usually rage within us, pulling us between good and evil, generosity and self-absorption, selflessness and narcissism.

Almost eight hundred years later, Rabbi Joseph Soloveitchik, too, described the sanctuary of teshuva and how it envelops us on these holiest of days:

> Jews do confess, but confession is a private matter between the individual and the Almighty. In my opinion, this is because of

> the Jew's typical modesty and shyness. The noblest and most exalted feelings that the Jew experiences must remain like the Ark of the Covenant, concealed behind the curtain. "And the curtain shall separate for you between the holy and the Holy of Holies" (Exodus 26:33). The sanctuary of the human person is his emotional life, not his logical life. The Ark is with us in each person's emotional life, concealed behind the curtain.[1]

Sometimes this Ark is so concealed that it is not always easy to locate our sanctuary of repentance. Even though we may be painfully aware of the need to change, we may lack the tools, the resilience, or the commitment to take on the demons of a difficult past or the challenges that come with the future. Rabbi Jonah was deeply concerned with those who put off the process of change and improvement, believing that such individuals only intensify their own problems: "Deferment of repentance is found only among the ignorant, who lie asleep and do not commune with their hearts, and who possess neither the knowledge nor the understanding to hasten to save themselves."[2] Those who know how to repent are those who can commune with their hearts, who can recognize with exquisite sensitivity where they are falling short of the mark. The rest of us lie asleep even when we are awake. We fail to save ourselves.

Rabbi Jonah offers us more than inspirational messages. To be effective, teshuva must move us all the way from regret to a place of profound change. The change must make us so distant from where we once were that we are actually able to instruct and guide others to avoid what was once a major source of personal temptation or spiritual weakness in ourselves. It is as if we were to look at an old photograph of ourselves. We recognize the image and the likeness but also know that we are not that same person anymore. Rabbi Jonah presents the anatomy of an apology as an outline for transformation in his table of contents, offering twenty steps that contribute to the process of true change.

- Experiencing regret
- Relinquishing sin
- Expressing sorrow
- Suffering

- Worrying
- Embodying shame
- Engaging in self-abasement
- Embracing humility in deed
- Conquering physical desire
- Improving deeds in relation to the sin
- Searching one's ways
- Recognizing the magnitude of sin
- Understanding the severity of lesser sins
- Confessing
- Praying
- Correcting the misdeed
- Pursuing acts of loving-kindness and truth
- Being aware of the constant presence of sin
- Forsaking the sin when temptation calls again
- Turning others away from sin

This list presents both the range of emotions that it takes to enter the sanctuary of repentance and the behavior that must emerge from these emotions. Sin, even of a minor ilk, must become magnified in our eyes so that we understand its cost and its consequences. The movement from sadness to sorrow to shame must be experienced, and that is only possible if we sit with our sins, analyzing their full impact – instead of briefly visiting them and then quickly squirreling them away. Humility is essential for a complete understanding of sin's influence. Without it, we may just write off the dimensions of a problem, not discovering its deeper causes and its far-reaching tentacles. The very last sentence in *The Gates of Repentance* is a verse from Psalms that captures the corrosive impact of sin: "The magnitude of sin is too heavy for me" (65:4). Sin weighs us down. It blocks us from moral advancement, chaining us to a stubborn soul, a recalcitrant heart.

Rabbi Jonah knew the process of teshuva intimately because he himself needed it. In 1233, Rabbi Jonah instigated a book-burning of Maimonides' most controversial work, *The Guide of the Perplexed*, in France. The Aristotelian overtones of the book felt foreign to many rabbis, and they worried about the impact this would have on the faith of their flocks. When twenty-four cartloads of handwritten volumes of the Talmud were put on trial in 1240 and then burned publicly in Paris two years later, Rabbi Jonah regretted his involvement in the initial book-burning. Rabbi Jonah seemed unable to forgive himself for condemning a great Jewish scholar, perhaps believing that this paved the way for future ecclesiastically driven book-burnings and anti-Semitic acts.

As penance, legend has it, Rabbi Jonah cited Maimonides in every one of his teachings and planned to enact an ancient Jewish custom: he intended to go to Maimonides' grave in Tiberias and bring a quorum to beg for Maimonides' forgiveness. He had already publicly acknowledged the error of his ways in his synagogue. He could not write about teshuva without practicing it. He could not describe and chastise the willful ignorance of those who did not improve themselves when he himself felt guilty of betrayal. He set off on the trip but was detained along the way and died of a rare illness in 1263; some attribute his illness to the fateful day that he assigned Maimonides' work to the flames. He knew he had to make amends, yet Rabbi Jonah never carried out the ritual to externalize the anguish he carried inside by making his apology in the presence of the offended and the community. Like so many of us, he knew what he had to do to right his error, but he only embarked on the journey. He did not complete it.

There are many activities we do this season to externalize sin so that we can be emboldened enough to conquer it. In the ancient days of the Bible, Yom Kippur was a time when two goats were designated by lottery to bear the sins of the people. One was to be sacrificed to achieve expiation and the other was, according to rabbinic tradition, to be dashed off a cliff, carrying to its death the weight of our collective transgressions. The ceremony must have been freighted with a degree of momentousness and nervous anticipation:

> Aaron shall lay both his hands upon the head of the live goat and confess over it all the iniquities and transgressions of the Israelites, whatever their sins, putting them on the head of the goat; and it shall be sent off to the wilderness through a designated man. Thus the goat shall carry on it all their iniquities to an inac-

> cessible region; and the goat shall be set free in the wilderness. (Leviticus 16:21–22)

Although in talmudic interpretations the goat met its death, in the biblical text the goat was merely shunted to an inaccessible region, a stunning metaphor for the abandonment of sin. We cannot kill the past; we can only hope that it travels to an inaccessible place where it no longer tempts, marks, or harms us.

The modern equivalent is the *tashlikh* ceremony where we ritually rid ourselves of sin by giving it to innocent fish. Alternatively, we may swing a chicken around our heads or palm our sins onto coins in its place. Some years ago, I found sin towelettes and a line of soaps designed to scrub us clean of all iniquity, following the reasoning at the end of the Leviticus chapter about the two goats: "This day of atonement shall be made for you to cleanse you of all your sins; you shall be clean before the Lord" (Leviticus 16:30). This verse suggested to the halakhic mind that the day of Yom Kippur itself has cleansing powers. Today you can even purchase pre-written apology notes where you check off the boxes that list your crimes and misdemeanors, conveniently providing the language of contrition if words are hard to conjure. I know all about the notes because I got one last year from a family member. In many ways, however, our attempts to externalize and remove sin have become shallow practices that distract us from the harder work of change. Teshuva-lite does not transform anyone; it only creates a ritual patina that may or may not stimulate repentance. Teshuva is not that easy.

In the introduction to his commentary on the Rosh HaShana *Maḥzor*, Rabbi Jonathan Sacks points out that teshuva means that our past does not dictate our future.[3] Rabbi Jonah believed that, too, and actively worked to overcome a wrong he had done in the past. That requires strength of character, as all authentic change does, and Rabbi Sacks elaborates on how important this drive is, especially during this season:

> Our determination to grow as human beings – our commitment to a more faithful, sensitive, decent life in the year to come –

> gives us the courage and honesty to face our past and admit its shortcomings. Our teshuva and God's forgiveness together mean that we are not prisoners of the past, held captive by it. *In Judaism sin is what we do, not what we are.*[4]

When sin is reduced to an act or a behavior rather than a state of being, repentance becomes instantly more manageable. Teshuva is not a journey in this framework. Ultimately, it is a destination. It is about reaching an outcome, even if the result sometimes eludes us – often more so the nearer we come to it. We are almost there. We have almost forgiven ourselves or asked the forgiveness of others. We have tried to close the chasm that exists between our Creator and ourselves. We come close. But then we regress. We walk backwards.

We discover that the process of change is not linear. Nor is it simple. It feels harder than anything we have ever done before. The enigma that repentance can feel both easy and difficult at times may be understood through the dichotomy that Rabbi Kook uses in *The Lights of Repentance* regarding specific and general teshuva. When it comes to specific transgressions, we can usually tackle them head-on. We know what the problem is, and we strive to find a solution and implement it. Teshuva, in this equation, is a relatively clear act of problem-solving. General teshuva, for Rabbi Kook, is more elusive. We cannot pinpoint any specific errors but live with a general feeling, like a spiritual malaise, that we are remote from God and that we are not acting as ourselves. Repenting for this type of problem is harder because it does not have the same clear-cut quality as specific repentance.

Perhaps because it is harder than anything else, teshuva, for Rabbi Kook, contains the possibility of dramatization. He wrote that "the inner pain of repentance is a great theme for the poets of sorrow to strike up upon their harps and for artists of tragedy – to thereby reveal their talent."[5] Repentance is the great dramatic narrative besetting all relationships. In that spirit, Michael Lavigne opens his novel, *Not Me,* with a contemporary father and son estrangement story. Michael, a middle-aged stand-up comedian, was in a marriage that crumbled, taking with it his one son. Michael's father, Heschel Rosenheim, is an aging Holocaust survivor who was once an upstanding member of the Jewish community but is now in the late stages of Alzheimer's disease. But Michael discovers that his father was never a Holocaust survivor; he was actually an SS officer who, to save his own life at the time of liberation, tattooed numbers onto his arm, traveled to Israel, and, ironically, ended up defending the country. On his deathbed, with his last breath Michael's father cries out, "Forgive me! God in heaven forgive me."[6] As Michael looks at his lifeless father, he is filled with pity. He sees no expected darkness, only light. Michael then makes some of his own observations about teshuva:

> I found it so hard to believe any of it really happened. How could a person change from one thing to its direct opposite, as if becoming someone else is as easy as changing your tie? And yet, what if it were true? What if he had been in the SS and on kibbutz and served in the Palmach and was a hero of the War of Independence and through pain and loss finally achieved some sort of capacity for love?
>
> I remembered how once he tried to explain to me the meaning of repentance. I was playing with the fringes of his long, elegant tallis. He smiled down at me.
>
> "In Hebrew," he said, "it means turning. Better, it means returning. It means to come back, Mikey, to come back to your true self." And then he laughed and pinched my nose. "And what could be easier than that?"
>
> "So why do we have to do it every year?"
>
> "Because, my dear little one, there is no one true self. And that is why repentance can never end."[7]

Teshuva is a never-ending process because we are always changing and the context of our universe is always shifting. This does not mean that there is no stable or true self – to disagree with Heschel Rosenheim; we know when we are being true to ourselves. We need multiple opportunities for teshuva because our mistakes and errors change over time, and our circumstances are fluid. The self is not static and unchanging, even if our essential personalities may be well established. Events change us. Relationships change us. Decisions change us. Life changes us. Therefore, there can never be an end to the process of teshuva.

In an exercise in which participants in a leadership class were asked to describe themselves in six words, most selected six adjectives and read them like a laundry-list of personality traits. Only one person in the group strung six words into a sentence: "Always do the right thing. Period." That decision to do the right thing – period – is how we interact with a world that keeps throwing challenges at us when we have a strong moral core. We can lose our way and be distant from God, from others, and from ourselves – but we can recover.

We commonly translate the word "teshuva" as repentance, from the Latin *pentir*, to feel sorrow, or *paenitere*, to be sorry or to regret. The latter is actually closer to our word *niḥam*, to regret or to experience remorse. We find this exact meaning early in Genesis, when God rethinks the nature of creation before the flood: "And God *regretted* that He had made man on earth, and His heart was saddened" (6:6). In this one verse, there is raw emotion; the sorrow generates regret. In Greek, this same idea is captured in the word *metanoia*, a combination of *meta* – after, and *noeo* – to think or to perceive. Repentance here is a reflection on the consequences of a bad decision, action, or judgment. We sin. We regret. Herein lies the feeling that underlies repentance, but it is not repentance itself. It is a change of heart or mind that immediately *precedes* a change of behavior. It is the raising of consciousness of sin and its after-effects. According to Jewish law, genuine teshuva cannot exist without this sentiment, but the feeling alone is not enough. Regret may change the future. It may not.

Shuv, on the other hand, is the action that follows the regret; it is the slow process of reverse. Regret teaches us how to return. It is the best trigger to change. *Niḥam* is regret; *shuv* is return. Why not capture repentance with a Hebrew word for change or transformation? What are we returning to when we return? I believe the language signifies the most profound possible meaning of repentance in Jewish life. It is not about change alone; it is about returning to the best self that one can be, acknowledging that every person has already achieved transcendence at some point, that we all know who we are when we are our best selves. We know what that looks and feels like. Now we have to recapture it.

For this reason, perhaps a change of English translation can shift the way we understand what we are doing when we repent and why. *Lashuv* means to return, but it can also mean to recover. We find this meaning, for example, in a variation of the word in I Samuel when David challenged a group of warring Amalekites. The enemy had killed the men of a city and then kidnapped its women and children, stealing possessions liberally. David was at the height of his power at the time and did not take this military escalation lightly. He attacked the Amalekites, showing his military prowess, and recovered every single item that was forcibly taken: "Nothing of theirs was missing – young or old, sons or daughters, spoil or anything else that had been carried off – David recovered [*heishiv*] everything" (30:19). As if every item taken were in some impressive inventory, David could have checked it all off at the end of the skirmish. Everything was back in its proper place, recovered and returned to its rightful owner.

Recovery is a powerful English word, capturing the emotion of returning in its grandest sense. When we ache with regret and distance from those we love, a paltry sorry alone will not recover what we have lost. In our relationships, we can say sorry and even mean it, but the road to the full recovery of a formerly warm state of affection and admiration can still be difficult to locate. We may see the sanctuary of repentance before us but not be able to find the door. We may have said the words of repentance but not bought in fully to all of its emotional demands. We may have regretted but not recovered, apologized but not actualized a new and improved relationship. Repentance requires that we love no less, and possibly more, than we did before the distance set in. It is not the sorry that is critical in this definition of teshuva, but rather the words and the deeds *after* the sorry, the positive commitment to intimacy we deliberatively create instead of allowing a bad mood to set in for the long haul. This is unlike the cold, formalized language of contrition that has little impact on thawing the remoteness that settles in between two people who want to make up but cannot get past their private wounds. They say the words to each other, but the feelings are still icy. The words come out all wrong. We've all been there before. Maybe we're there now.

The same King David who recovered property that was taken and returned it had a harder time mustering recovery in his relationship with his son Avshalom, as told in II Samuel. Avshalom nursed hatred for his half-brother Amnon for the rape of his sister Tamar. Two years after the rape, Avshalom killed Amnon in revenge and then fled in fear. David and his royal court mourned Amnon. Through this difficult mourning period, Avshalom stayed away from his father for three years. The relationship was frozen with grief and loss. "But King David was pining away for Avshalom, for the king had gotten over Amnon's death" (13:39). As time passed and healed one wound, another was reopened. David longed to recover his relationship with his estranged son Avshalom, but he could not bring himself to forgive him or configure a noble way to create an encounter. Yoav, David's nephew and a captain of his army, saw through the pain and devised a ruse to bring father and son together. He found a woman in Tekoa, dressed her in the robes of mourning, and asked her to visit the king with a request. This unnamed woman on a mission of mercy fell prostrate before the king and cried out to him. David wanted to know how to help. She told her tale of woe. Her husband died, and her two sons came to blows. One killed the other, and now the clan wanted the remaining son to be put to death, wiping out her only heir. Her son was all she had left in her diminished universe; she wanted his life to be spared. The king agreed.

If the king was not able to see through the case and into the mirror, the woman from Tekoa made the message explicit, asking the king if she could utter yet another word. She told the king with words of existential despair that he was mistaken not to bring back his own banished son: "We must all die; we are like water that is poured on the ground and cannot be gathered up" (14:14). Mistakes happen. Life is short. Forgiveness endures. Love is possible. It is time to put the past behind.

The king asked the stranger before him if she had been sent by Yoav. The woman from Tekoa told the truth. Yoav had indeed put her up to this, but only because Yoav saw that the king needed to make peace with his son but could not find a way to do so while maintaining his pride and dignity. We often want to resolve a conflict but are not willing enough to squelch a bloated ego and say sorry. David needed the relationship to recover. Yoav found a way; the king commanded Yoav to bring Avshalom home.

Sadly, the story does not end here. Even once Avshalom was brought directly to his home, King David would not see him for two years. For two years, the two souls hovered in Jerusalem without a sighting. Avshalom lost his patience, burned one of Yoav's fields to get his attention, and then complained that his father David refused to see him. If he was guilty, he was prepared to die, but he wanted to know his crime. Yoav reported this to the king and then summoned Avshalom to the palace. "He came to the king and flung himself to the ground before the king. And the king kissed Avshalom" (14:33).

We find ourselves in this moment of tenderness with a father and his estranged son. We feel the ground beneath Avshalom when he threw himself to the floor and the intimacy of David's kiss when Avshalom picked himself up. We recognize the pain intermingled with joy offered by a moment of recovery.

Yet strained relationships take a lot more than a kiss to heal. So much time had elapsed – five years – that the tension between father and son never fully recovered. Perhaps the work needed for recovery was never complete. Avshalom, in the next chapters of II Samuel, began to threaten the throne and set himself up as an alternate ruler. While there may have been regret and an apology – we do not know what was said – it was evidently not enough.

David's story reminds us that if we believe teshuva can be achieved in one day of intense prayer, we will never really understand what teshuva truly demands of us: full and total recovery. In the biblical story it takes years and is still not fully achieved. Recovery is a process, not a singular act. It requires tenderness, commitment, and patience. Yom Kippur may represent the beginning of the process, but it is rarely its end.

I write this on the day after Yom Kippur, the most solemn day of the Jewish calendar, thinking of Yom Kippur a year from now. Yom Kippur lingers. It lingers in my mind, prompting heightened consciousness of wrongdoing, an attenuated sense of rectitude and gratitude. Ah, the gift of being alive. Of living another year. Of having the spiritual stamina to make it to the end of *Ne'ila*, the day's closing prayer.

Yom Kippur also lingers in my body, which takes a few days to recover from the shock and physicality of fasting. There are two fasts in Jewish law in the same week, and I always marvel at how I can fast for two out of seven days and still manage to gain weight. Fasting makes material demands of us, as it should. R. Elazar, in the Talmud, remarked that fasting is greater than charity, and explained himself: fasting is accomplished through one's person while charity is only accomplished through one's possessions.[8] Fasting is meant to linger.

But Yom Kippur also lingers in my heart, warping it with the intensity of my mortality. It is the day that helps me frequent death. Not a year passes when I do not say its central prayer, *Unetaneh Tokef*, as tears flow fast and furiously down my face and drop unglamorously from the tip of my nose into my prayerbook. "Who will die a timely death and who will die an untimely death. Who by fire and who by water...." I am absolutely dumbstruck by the haphazard and drunken way that the Angel of Death has extracted people from my congregation: this one's wife to cancer, this one's daughter to suicide, that one's father in an accident. And I don't cry only because I am afraid of judgment (although, no doubt, I should). I cry because I am frightened to death of death and its seeming randomness and my incapacity to ever see a larger master plan. I am terrified of the possibility that I will not live long enough to see grandchildren, to travel, to grow old with my husband. I will die and others will live in the shadow of my death, like the magician pulling the tablecloth but leaving all of the teacups trembling in their places. I am frightened by all the hurt that death creates in its wake, by the thought that my death will cause pain to others. More: I am afraid to lose someone I love. Did I dare utter that, form words that may, God forbid, precipitate that reality?

Yom Kippur is supposed to be a miniature death. We enter the universe of death as the sun sets and the fast begins. We confess on our deathbeds; we confess one day a year. We wear white shrouds in the coffin; we wear white one day a year. We do not need shoes for our ultimate journey; we don't wear them one day a year. We cannot participate in the acts that make us alive before we breathe our last; we refrain from our most human, material needs one day a year. On Yom Kippur we imitate death so that we may truly live.

And precisely because we wait for the heavy shoe of tragedy to drop and spoil and soil the abundant goodness we have unfairly come to expect as our due do we leave Yom Kippur more alive than we have ever been. We know that all the majesty of our lives will be taken away one day and that makes every moment we are here more worthwhile. As I pray on Yom Kippur, I am aware of my absolute smallness in a universe I will never understand. I wonder at the odd paradox of how prayer crushes the ego in its grab for transcendence. Stoop low. Push higher. There is an elegance to humility, the slow punch of its descents and ascents.

On Rosh HaShana we acknowledge God's majesty and authority in the universe. We realize that we must abandon the illusion that we have ultimate control; we must soften the tight grip we falsely believe we have over the future. On Yom Kippur we mimic death, the ultimate statement that we have no control over our mortality. The confrontation with death prompts us to reconsider what we've been living for. We spend the days in between in a state of vulnerability; on the day after Yom Kippur we take greater control of ourselves and what we need to achieve. We lose control to gain control.

We have these ten days – the *Asseret Yemei Teshuva* – to pray, to cry, to improve, to change, to forgive, to apologize, to become what we've always meant to become, to return, to come home, to build the sanctuary that is repentance. We have these ten days to recover, to revisit our best selves, to become whole again. And each day that we fail in this task, we must pick ourselves up again with the reminder: "Once more with feeling." There is always tomorrow.

LIFE HOMEWORK

Think of one relationship you are in that needs recovery. Imagine the relationship's most tender moments and the time when the person meant a great deal to you, and ask yourself why. What would it take to return to that place of affection or admiration? What is getting in the way? How are *you* getting in the way?

It is at this time of year that our greatest personal insecurities typically surface. We feel remote from ourselves. Instead of pushing these powerful insecurities away, invite some of them into heightened view. Consider a time when you felt really good about the person you were. What would it take to return to that place of affection or admiration? What is getting in the way? How are *you* getting in the way of your best self?

Having imagined what recovery might look like with another human being and with yourself, now imagine a time when your relationship with God was at a high point, a spiritual apex. What would it take to return to that place of affection or admiration? What is getting in the way? How are *you* getting in the way?

Notes

1. Rabbi Joseph Soloveitchik, from his lecture "The Abridged Havinenu Prayer" at the Rabbinic Council of America Midwinter Conference (Feb. 7, 1968); retold in Aaron Rakeffet-Rothkoff, *The Rav: The World of Rabbi Joseph B. Soloveitchik* (New York: Ktav, 1999), 2:167.
2. Rabbi Jonah, *The Gates of Repentance,* trans. Shraga Silverstein (Jerusalem: Feldheim Publishers, 1967), 5.
3. Rabbi Jonathan Sacks, *The Koren Rosh HaShana Maḥzor* (Jerusalem: Koren, 2011), xxvii.
4. Ibid. Italics are mine.
5. Rabbi Abraham Isaac Kook, *The Lights of Repentance,* trans. Alter B.Z. Metzger (New York: Yeshiva University Press, 1978), 52.
6. Michael Lavigne, *Not Me* (New York: Random House, 2007), 277.
7. Ibid., 278.
8. Berakhot 32b.

Day One

Faith

"For the sin we committed before You by throwing off the yoke of heaven."

On the first day of Rosh HaShana, our Torah reading is dominated by an unlikely character, a foreign servant woman who becomes a key player in the fertility struggle of Abraham and Sarah: Hagar. Her appearance takes us off guard. She receives not one chapter in the unfolding of Genesis, but two. The story of her promotion to wife and then first mother, followed by her sudden banishment, is painful and uncomfortable to read. She seems to be a pawn in a story far greater than herself. Her story strangely occupies a large emotional space in Abraham's narratives of faith, and it is reviewed on one of our most solemn liturgical occasions.

Hagar is introduced as an Egyptian maidservant with a name that means "stranger"; everything about her is remote and distant. She comes from elsewhere and occupies a low station in Abraham's household. Midrashim about her former position as princess notwithstanding, the text presents a woman with no status whatsoever. Hagar is introduced in our story only after Abraham has already toyed with possible solutions to his problem of an heir. Sarah's infertility is mentioned early on, when we first meet the future matriarch: "Now Sarai was barren, she had no child" (Genesis 11:30). By the time Abraham is tasked with creating a nation, the reader already understands the challenges ahead. As a first solution, Abraham takes his nephew Lot with him, and his name is mentioned in Abraham's travels to Canaan before Sarah's is. He is clearly regarded as the likely heir until the two parties have property skirmishes and separate. Abraham then asks God if his house servant Eliezer should be his heir, but God rejects this option. In Genesis 15, Abraham is told explicitly that the solution to his problem will come from his belly, literally: "None but your very own issue shall be your heir" (15:4). The child is to come from him. It will not be Lot. It will not be Eliezer. But the child will not necessarily be the offspring of Sarah, either, since it is Abraham's "womb" and not Sarah's that God specifies.

Perhaps Sarah overheard this conversation or it was reported to her; whatever precipitates her action, she decides at this juncture to take fate into her own hands. She gives her maidservant to Abraham. She does not perform this as an act of generosity to help her husband fulfill the divine promise of Genesis 12 that Abraham will father a nation. Each nation begins with one. And Abraham, try as he might, cannot come up with the first one. Genesis 16 explicitly states Sarah's motive in her own words: "Perhaps *I* shall have a son through her [lit. "be built up through her"]" (16:2). Abraham will get an heir, she reckons, as part of some larger divine scheme, but she chances not being part of this majestic, historic tale. Sarah has to act to guarantee her own place. Maybe, just maybe, she can have a son through surrogacy, solving her emotional anguish and also cementing her historic significance as the mother of a nation.

Sarah gives her maid over as a wife rather than a concubine, a term in rabbinic parlance that implies a wife but one without the financial security of a marriage contract. In doing this, Sarah changes Hagar's status monumentally, moving her from a subordinate figure in the household to one almost on par with herself. When Hagar gets pregnant and then ridicules Sarah, Hagar has, of her own accord, shifted the power balance again, lording her new position in the house as first mother over her former mistress. In actuality, Hagar could have belittled Sarah without much effort. Seeing Hagar's growing stomach is signal enough for Sarah to experience inadequacy. Phyllis Trible describes the changing scales of power in the Sarah/Hagar story beautifully in her book *Texts of Terror*:[1] a woman of little significance is suddenly moved to center stage, pushing aside the female protagonist who could not deliver.

Sarah's indignity at her sudden change in position is a source of outrage. She turns to Abraham with her humiliation: "The wrong done me is your fault! I myself put my maid in your bosom; now that she sees that she is pregnant, I am lowered in her esteem. The Lord decide between me and you!" (16:5). Sarah had thought she was helping the family with this arrangement, but she comes to realize the mistake of it all. In Sarah's failed attempt to build herself up through Hagar, she is ironically made small though her. The Bible commentator Rabbi Meir Leibush (1809–1879), known by the acronym Malbim, understood Hagar's dismissal of Sarah as linked to the fact that Hagar conceived immediately; one might think Hagar was more righteous than her mistress. Sarah blames her indignity on Abraham; perhaps his own happiness at becoming a father was too much for Sarah. Hagar's arrogance – or her very existence – becomes Sarah's new blight.[2] Sarah creates a challenge for Abraham. Rather than position herself against Hagar, Sarah gives Abraham a choice. He must choose a life with Sarah and her infertility, which means letting go of God's larger vision of Abraham's future, or choose the leadership role God determined for him, which he must pursue without her. Sarah can no longer see a way for Abraham to have his national, spiritual dream and to keep their relationship intact when she could not provide an heir.

Abraham, wise patriarch that he was, responds to Sarah's humiliation: "Your maid is in your hands. Deal with her as you think right" (16:6). This is Abraham's clever way of telling his wife that this plan was her idea, not his. He had no emotional attachment to Hagar; just as she easily shifted from being Sarah's maid to Abraham's wife, Hagar can shift back to her old role without Abraham being invested in her change of status. Then Abraham tells Sarah to do with Hagar as *she* deems right, returning to Sarah all the power she once had over this woman. There is irony in this statement. Sarah afflicts her maid, not knowing how to return this woman, pregnant with her husband's heir, back to her former role without the use of verbal or physical violence; we are unsure how exactly to read the postscript: "Sarah treated her harshly, and she ran away from her" (16:6). Having tasted a modicum of freedom, Hagar is not prepared to redress the new imbalance and return to the indignity of servitude.

This inverse story of Exodus, in which an Israelite enslaves an Egyptian, treats her harshly (using the same Hebrew terminology used to describe Pharaoh's oppression of the Israelites), and forces her to run off to the wilderness to escape, has a different end than our national narrative.[3] Hagar finds herself near a spring and encounters an angel. He tells her to return to her place of anguish even though she will suffer there, because she will birth her own nation, beginning with Abraham's first child, Ishmael. The child, the angel tells her, will be a "wild animal of a man; his hand against everyone and everyone's hand against him" (16:12). The promise of a child of violence hardly seems a motivation to return unless, of course, Hagar believes that as a powerless slave, this is her best chance for her own future defense. Finally her defenselessness can become her empowerment; she has recourse to combat violence with violence, all to fulfill a larger vision of a nation: her own. The angel presages the message with what must have seemed a preposterous promise: "I will greatly increase your offspring, and they will be too many to count" (16:10). Oddly, Hagar is the only woman in the Hebrew Bible to receive the female version of Abraham's blessing of multitudes. This promise unlocks the mystery of why we read Hagar's story on Rosh HaShana, one of our holiest days.

To understand the promise, we have to telescope forward to the text of Hagar that is included in our *Maḥzor*: Genesis 21. Ishmael is likely seventeen, on the cusp of adulthood; his half-brother Isaac is being celebrated by his parents. Isaac, the miracle child, has been weaned, and Abraham makes a large feast. With Isaac's viability, the issue of who will be Abraham's heir comes into peak narrative tension.[4] Sarah, at the height of her happiness, sees "the son whom Hagar the Egyptian had borne to Abraham playing" (21:9) and is reviled. Using a more subordinate Hebrew name for slave than was used in Genesis 16,[5] Sarah once again gives Abraham an unambiguous mandate: "Cast out that slave woman and her son, for the son of that slave shall not share in the inheritance with my son Isaac" (21:10). Neither son is called the child of Abraham; there is only the son of Hagar and the son of Sarah, pitted in Sarah's mind in an intense competition for succession. Now that Ishmael is an adult and technically fit to be heir, Sarah sees his playing as either an erotic danger (as posited in one midrash), a strange childish aberration for a young adult, or a status problem for her son. Banishing Ishmael would leave only one child behind, Isaac, as if the birthright were a matter of geographic accessibility. Where Abraham listened to his wife before without emotional investment, here the text renders his anguish: "Abraham was greatly distressed for it concerned a son of *his*" (21:12). Sarah may have easily cut out Abraham's role as father in discussing Ishmael, but Abraham could not. The child was also *his* child.

God tells Abraham to listen to his wife, and Abraham dutifully sends out Hagar and Ishmael into an unforeseen future in the wilderness. He gives Hagar bread and a skin of water, putting it on her shoulder – a last act of tenderness – and mother and son set off. Many medieval commentators on this story question Abraham's parsimony. When a slave was set free in the laws framed in Deuteronomy, he was entitled to more than this woman – who was first a slave and then a wife – received from her master/husband for her ignominious exit.

Then Hagar gets lost and her water runs out. In despair, she puts her child, now a man, under a bush, not wanting to see her son die, presumably of dehydration. She sits a bow's distance away and bursts into tears, but the angel this time only hears the weeping of the boy. The English rendering of the angel's words sounds compassionate: "What troubles you, Hagar?" (21:17). The Hebrew is more remonstrative: "What is the matter with you, Hagar?" These three Hebrew words contain the key to unraveling this text and Hagar's role in Abraham's story.

Hagar's behavior here provides an ancient literary foil to demonstrate the extent of Abraham's faith. Abraham is given a promise: to become a nation in a homeland. He is successful in his role as homesteader, amassing wealth and cattle, digging wells, fighting wars, and making covenants with neighboring peoples. But he struggles for more than a dozen chapters to make good on the pledge of a nation because he cannot produce even one heir. He finally has one child and then another, then banishes one child and then almost offers the other as a sacrifice, making him once again almost childless. He turns to God for guidance and direction, even when he stares into the abyss of ambiguity. God points him to a sky full of stars on several occasions with hopefulness, and Abraham never doubts Him despite immense confusion. Sarah sarcastically laughs at the promise of a child past her childbearing years. She doubts. Abraham, too, laughs, but it is a different laugh. It is the laughter of joy and relief, the chuffing of optimism. Hers is the laugh of disbelief. His is the laugh of faith.

Hagar was given the same promise as Abraham, to be the progenitor of a nation, but when a simple physical obstruction stands in her way, she balks. She puts her child of promise near a bush, expecting him to die. When the angel comes to her, he opens Hagar's eyes, and she beholds a well. The text does not say that God created a well, only that her eyes were opened, and she saw it for the first time. A solution lay right in front of her, but she lacked the ambition, the inspiration, or the faith to see it. Abraham, even when his vision was clouded, held on tightly to the promise and found the faith to surmount every obstacle until he achieved God's word. Hagar let go too soon.

We read Hagar's story nestled into Abraham's on Rosh HaShana to point to our own choices within the framework of faith and trust. Do we have the faith to hold on to a vision of a better future or does that vision collapse the moment something stands in the way? How strong is our faith? How determined are we to live a life of promise?

Hagar acted as an ordinary mother would have – but she had been given an extraordinary promise. Rather than nurture it with extraordinary determination, she let it go, opting for tears of self-pity. Self-pity is an easy place to visit. Hagar did have a very difficult life. But she also received a blessing of abundance that required effort and belief. She could not see that because she was overwhelmed by her powerlessness. A well lay before her – a reservoir of blessing in the ancient Near East – but she was blind to it. And when we read how quickly Hagar gave up on a divine promise, we become more awed by the fact that Abraham never gave up despite problems much more significant than those faced by his wife's former slave. If we could not understand why Søren Kierkegaard called Abraham a knight of faith before we read Genesis 21, we understand the philosopher now.

Sometimes we fall in love with our problems. They become us. We cannot live without the drama. We are too restless to appreciate the abundance that God has given us and instead of bowing deeply for *Modim* (prayer of gratitude), we are stuck in one long *Taḥanun* (supplication of lowliness). Our problems give us something to talk about and someone else to blame. We see problems recurring when a situation does not change but do not necessarily take responsibility for changing it. We do not accept our own complicit role in our problems. It was easy enough for Hagar to blame Abraham for not giving her enough water to sustain her, for sending her away, for making her a helpless player in a narrative far larger than herself. It is easy enough to sit down and cry and become so entangled in a problem that we don't even think about how to change it. We can all do that. We blame others. We blame God. But it does not advance us. Blame was not going to save Ishmael, and it is not going to save us.

Faith demands patience in the face of a future that we cannot see and the determination to make good things happen. If we could know the future with certainty, we would not need faith. But because we cannot know, we have to trust in powers greater than ours to guide us. Our faith is not the passive faith of Hagar's tears but the active joy of Abraham's laugh. We admire his propulsion forward, his drive to create an ambitious, dream-worthy vision even if all of the particulars comprising that future were beyond his immediate understanding. Faith demands that we engage in a delicate dance of both relinquishing control to an authority above us and acting within our full human capacity to realize our dreams.

On Rosh HaShana we celebrate God's kingship by acknowledging God's authority. We recommit ourselves to being faithful servants of the king. A faithful servant does not wait for a better future but, in partnership, creates one.

LIFE HOMEWORK

Abraham's faith demanded a contradictory blend of patience and impatience. Sometimes we need more patience to actualize ourselves and to make situations better. Sometimes we need impatience to achieve the same ends. We allow a situation to stay the same or fester because we do not take charge of shaping it. Wisdom demands that we know when to be patient and when to be impatient. Rosh HaShana offers us the opportunity to think about our own state of faith in the coming year. Ask yourself:

- Where in your life do you need to be more patient? What will you do to express that patience in the future?
- Where in your life do you need to be more impatient? What will you do to express that impatience in the future?

PASSAGES FOR ADDITIONAL STUDY

Maimonides, *Mishneh Torah, The Laws of Repentance* 1:3

> At present, when the Temple does not exist and there is no altar of atonement, there remains nothing else aside from teshuva. Teshuva atones for all sins. Even a person who was wicked his whole life and repented in his final moments will not be reminded of any aspect of his wickedness, as Ezekiel [33:12] states: "The wickedness of the evil one will not cause him to stumble on the day he repents his wickedness." The essence of Yom Kippur atones for those who repent, as Leviticus [16:30] states: "This day will atone for you."

Rabbi Moshe Haim Luzzatto, *The Path of the Just*, Chapter 1: "Concerning Man's Duty in the World"

> The foundation of saintliness and the root of perfection in the service of God lies in a man's coming to see clearly and to recognize as a truth the nature of his duty in the world and the end towards which he should direct his vision and his aspiration in all of his labors all the days of his life.

Rabbi Abraham Isaac Kook, *The Lights of Repentance* 8:8

> When the anguish, which is the pain of penitence brought about by the person's own spiritual state and that of the whole world, becomes very great, to a point of blocking the creative sources of thought, speech, prayer, outcries, feeling and song, then one must rise in a leap to seek life-giving lights in the source of silence. "The parched land will become a pool, and the thirsty ground springs of water." (Isaiah 35:7)

Text questions to think about while studying:

- How does the importance of faith affect the process of repentance?
- How does a broader vision of the future change the present?
- What kind of anxieties hold us back from change?

Notes

1. Phyllis Trible, *Texts of Terror: Literary-Feminist Readings of Biblical Narratives* (Philadelphia: Fortress Press, 1985), 9–35.
2. For more on this, see Jo Ann Hackett, "Rehabilitating Hagar: Fragments of an Epic Pattern," in *Gender and Difference in Ancient Israel,* ed. Peggy L. Day (Minneapolis: Fortress Press, 1989), 12–19.
3. For mention of this narrative within others that also bear Exodus themes and language, see David Daube, *The Exodus Pattern in the Bible* (London: Faber and Faber, 1963).
4. For more on this, see Naomi Steinberg, "The Sarah-Hagar Cycle: Polycoity," in *Kinship and Marriage in Genesis: A Household Economics Perspective* (Minneapolis: Fortress Press, 1993), 35–86.
5. For a discussion of the difference between a *shifḥa* and an *ama* in Hebrew, see F. Charles Fensham, "The Son of a Handmaid in Northwest-Semitic," *Vetus Testamentum* 19:3 (July, 1969), 312–321.

Day Two

Destiny

"For the sin we committed before You with a confused heart."

Rosh HaShana has its tastes, sounds, and texts. We think of symbolic food like pomegranates and apples dipped in honey. We hear the *shofar*'s call for mercy and we revisit texts that are central to our tradition. One of them, the most difficult of them, is the binding of Isaac. It is in this text that both sound and time merge almost seamlessly. At once, we encounter the text, close our eyes, and mythically hear the ram's horn that we imagine Abraham might have blown as a testament to his loyalty to God.

Unexpectedly, the biblical chapter that brought us the first *shofar*'s blast is awkwardly quiet. In the binding of Isaac narration there is neither crying nor supplication. There are no petitions for mercy and no explanations. There is little noise. The silence of the nineteen verses that tell the story is overpowering. God asked something of Abraham with initially one word only: "Abraham." Abraham responded, in kind, with one word: "*Hineni*." I am fully present and at Your command. It is as if

Abraham had said, "My name is my destiny. Call it, and I will accept Your will." And he did. Although God explained the task in limited detail, the test was essentially delivered in one word. Abraham's "*Hineni*" followed his name, not the description of the test that stood before him.

A few verses later, we find another almost wordless conversation of a similar kind. Isaac, too, called Abraham, but this time not by name but by role: "Father." And to Isaac, Abraham also said "*Hineni*," followed by the most painful word in the chapter "*beni*," my son. With one son banished in the previous chapter and another about to be taken on a mountain altar of undisclosed location, Abraham would not have many chances to address his son again. The word must have dropped to the ground like a heavy weight.

Isaac wanted to know where the sheep was for the offering since the wood and the fire implement were in place. Isaac carried the wood. Abraham carried the fire starter and the knife. Isaac conveniently forgot to inquire about the knife in his description of their readiness. It was not an ordinary knife. A "*ma'akhelet*" – from the Hebrew word to consume – is found in only one other place in the Hebrew Bible, in a text that makes readers shudder: chapter 19 of Judges. The knife Abraham used in Genesis and the one used in the Concubine of Givah text was used specifically to cut human flesh, not an act generally done within our faith tradition. No wonder poor Isaac forgot to mention it. Abraham explained their three-day sojourn together to Isaac in six truthful but elusive Hebrew words: "God will see to the sheep for His burnt offering, my son." Again, the words "my son" end Abraham's sentence with an ominous thud. The two proceed in silence.

Abraham said "*Hineni*" one more time, after an angel called his name twice to stay his knife-wielding hand. It took one mention of Abraham's name to begin his mission but two to stop it. Abraham looked up, trying to find a replacement for the child he never sacrificed. Although the narrative is all about following directions, and although Abraham stated unambiguously that God would show them the sheep for sacrifice, it was actually Abraham who identified the animal. It was a ram. "When Abraham looked up, his eye fell upon a ram caught in the thicket by its horns. Abraham offered it up as a burnt offering in place of his son" (Genesis 22:13). And then, in the biblical tradition of renaming a location after an act of divine revelation, Abraham renamed the place where he stood: "And Abraham named that site Adonai-yireh, as it is called to this day 'On the mount of the Lord there is vision'" (22:14).

Abraham saw a ram, yet he named the mount after God's long-term vision, not his own immediate vision. Abraham had passed the final test of his loyalty and, in so doing, praised the God who did *not* ask him to sacrifice his son. There was a vision on that mount that was unlike anything else Abraham knew of the ultimate sacrifices demanded in other ancient Near Eastern faiths. It was as if God said to Abraham through the slow pace of the narration and its silence: "Know forevermore that this new faith will be a radical departure from whatever you know. It will never demand child sacrifice as surrounding faiths do. Instead it will demand ultimate trust, and that you have earned on this mountain today."[1] Although Abraham was not asked to offer an animal, perhaps he saw in that ram stuck in the thicket – a place of entrapment and pain – the symbolic representation of a life full of struggle that was finally easing.

For Abraham, the binding was about sight. For us, Abraham's descendants, the binding is about sound. Abraham experienced a vision and named the place after that vision. He did not blow the ram's horn on that mountain – or, if he did, there is no recording of it. But somehow, the sound of the *shofar* – so primitive and so plaintive – echoes in Jewish history for all time and has always been associated with this story. A midrash on the sound of the *shofar* in the transmission of the Ten Commandments in Exodus 20 advances the idea that the same *shofar* was used at both Moriah and Sinai, presaging one person's commitment of faith into that of an entire nation through a sound associated with mountain heights and divine authority.

The mystery of this instrument of faith was not lost on the rabbis of old. In a beautiful midrash on Genesis 22, the sages hold forth on the *shofar*'s reach, taking us to the very day of its first use:

> Throughout that day, Abraham saw the ram become entangled in a tree, break loose and go free, become entangled in a bush, break loose and go free; then again become entangled in a thicket, break loose and go free. The Holy One said, "Abraham, so will your

> children be entangled in many kinds of sin and trapped within successive kingdoms – from Babylon to Media, from Media to Greece, from Greece to Rome." Abraham asked, "Master of the Universe, will it be forever thus?" God replied, "In the end they will be redeemed by [the sound of] the horn of this ram." (Genesis Rabba on Genesis 22:13)

For Abraham, the *shofar* was never about a sound. It was predominantly about a sight. Abraham saw an animal that symbolized himself, his son, and his fledgling nation, a ram that had difficulty negotiating its environs. It became entangled. It broke free. This pattern repeated itself.

Looking at this image, Abraham realized the metaphor unfolding before his eyes. But unlike his conclusion, God drew another from it that involved sound. When the *shofar* is blown, it always signals redemption to those who hear it – whether it is at Mount Sinai with the giving of the law or when slaves were freed in ancient days. The *shofar* may look like entanglement – but the *shofar* sounds like freedom.

We cannot envision what it was like for Abraham or for Isaac to be on that mountain that day. The closest we can come to reenacting that moment of faith is by closing our eyes and imagining a *shofar* being blown into the wind on the top of a mountain; it is the loneliest sound imaginable. That *shofar*'s wail released all of the tears that were not shed on that day and all of the cries that were never emitted and all of the words that went unsaid. The anguish and the victory of it all is captured most potently with the primitive, primal scream of a *shofar*.

When the *shofar* is blown on Rosh HaShana, all time collapses. We revisit our master story again and again, understanding that we are part of an ancient, treasured history, one of entanglement and also of redemption. The problem is to know when we are stuck and when we are just at the beginning of a breakthrough. Often the very same moment can appear to be both. We mistake trouble for possibility or do not see harm or temptation right ahead. Abraham saw a ram in a thicket, a live creature stuck in brambles. He offered up this animal as a testimony to a moment when he was ready to give one thing but was asked for another instead. His destiny could have taken one turn. Instead it took another.

Destiny does not always introduce itself. We have a chance encounter that ends up changing our lives because we are able to say at a moment's notice, "*Hineni*." I am here. I am ready. Nahmanides understood that the verb *nisa* – and God tested Abraham – was fate calling Abraham to a test that God knew he could pass. Challenging tests of character common in the world of Greek gods and heroes helped the protagonist understand his own mettle, offering an affirmation of strength and pointing to a fate often unanticipated. A strange moment or obstacle suddenly becomes the beginning of a new and unexpected journey that becomes the journey of a lifetime.

This message of destiny and its enigmatic turns underlines much of our Rosh HaShana liturgy and fills the pages of the *Maḥzor*. The *haftara* on the first day of Rosh HaShana (1 Samuel 1:1–2:10) affirms the role of fate and destiny in a plan we cannot totally fathom. After bringing her son Samuel to the Tabernacle as a servant for life following an emotional battle with infertility, Hannah offers a prayer. Surprisingly, it is not a prayer of thanksgiving but one that captures the seeming arbitrariness of a world of fate:

> Then Hannah prayed and said, "My heart rejoices in the Lord; in the Lord my horn is lifted high. My mouth boasts over my enemies, for I delight in Your deliverance. There is no one holy like the Lord; there is no one besides You; there is no Rock like our God. Do not keep talking so proudly or let your mouth speak such arrogance, for the Lord is a God who knows, and by Him deeds are weighed. The bows of the warriors are broken, but those who stumbled are armed with strength. Those who were full hire themselves out for food, but those who were hungry hunger no more. She who was barren has borne seven children, but she who has had many sons pines away. The Lord brings death and makes alive; He brings down to the grave and raises up. The Lord sends poverty and wealth; He humbles and He exalts. He raises the poor from the dust and lifts the needy from the ash heap; He seats them with princes and has them inherit a throne of honor. For the foundations of the earth are the Lord's; upon them He has set the world." (1 Samuel 2:1–8)

The prayer continues, but its message is already clear. Those who are poor may find themselves rich one day. Women who have no children may find themselves mothers one day. Warriors stumble. The needy sit with princes. Life as we know it is incomprehensible to the limitations of the human mind. Forces beyond our ken take over, and life as we know it changes dramatically.

James Kugel captures this oddity of fate and destiny in his essay "A Moment of Confusion" from *The God of Old*.[2] Encounters with angels in the Bible, says Kugel, often begin as seemingly coincidental visits between human beings. Abraham saw three guests passing his tent in the distance. They were actually angels who, after a time of sustaining normalcy, disclosed their real identities and predicted an entirely new path ahead for Abraham and his wife. After dozens of years of infertility, this couple would become parents, and the small nation they founded would have its first successor. Abraham was only the first of many to transition from one dimension to another in a human/angel encounter. Human beings in the ancient world, according to Kugel, navigated spiritual worlds in ways that modern human beings do not. They may not have recognized an angel before them, but they were not shocked by such meetings either. The transition from this-worldly to other-worldly was not staggering or dramatic but almost expected. There was a readiness to move within a dimension not visible. At any time, three angels might show up at your door with a message that could change your life for eternity. A bush might burn in flames but not be consumed. A sea might split when you stand on the cusp of its shore with hundreds of enemy chariots directly behind you. A moment of confusion turns into a moment of revelation without the skip of a heartbeat or the time to catch a breath.

You were about to do something that would change your life forever when an angel stayed your hand. At first you were confused, but you moved slowly enough to stop yourself, and in so doing, retrieved what you thought you were about to lose: the most important relationship in your life.

Confusion collapses into clarity.

We confess to confusion on Yom Kippur: "*For the sin we committed before You with a confused heart.*" How can confusion ever be a sin?

It is not intentional. Confusion is not an act; it is a condition brought about by the ambiguities of a situation. But we can perpetuate confusion by not seeking clarity soon enough or at all. And for that, we confess. Confusion can do that to us. In the prayerbook of the Vilna Gaon, Rabbi Elijah Kramer (1720–1796), this plea includes acts of wrongdoing connected with confusion: doubting principles of faith or law or wondering about the historic existence of prophets or the reliability of Jewish texts. It can also be connected to the pain or anguish we cause ourselves and others because of doubt.

We stay in a state of confusion by not recognizing that destiny does not always knock on our door and announce itself. We have to ready ourselves for a moment as sudden as the appearance of a ram in a thicket, as sudden as the answer to a prayer of infertility.

What will you answer when destiny knocks?

Hineni.

Don't miss the moment.

LIFE HOMEWORK

A sign on a church lawn read: "Negativity delays divine destiny."

Fate comes looking for us, but sometimes we are looking down and cannot see possibility. We find ourselves saying "no" to opportunities. The *hineni* moment passes us by. Rosh HaShana offers us the beginning of a new year to take risks and step outside of our comfort zones and grow. Think of one thing you said "no" to in the recent past. What would it look like to revisit it and say "yes"?

In the Talmud, Rabbi Eleazar, a scholar at the Academy of Yavneh during the first century of the Common Era, said, "No is an oath, and yes is an oath." Rava said an oath is only compelling if fully emphasized: "Only if one said, 'no, no' twice or 'yes, yes' twice."[3] Sometimes a "yes" or a "no" is not an honest answer. Rabbi Moshe Haim Luzzatto, basing himself on a commentary on Leviticus 19:36, wrote, "Your 'no' should be righteous, and your 'yes' should be righteous."[4] A righteous "no" or a righteous "yes" is an honest reply when righteousness implies integrity and objectivity. Watch yourself in the next few days with these two words alone.

Exercise 1:

Is your "yes" righteous?
Is your "no" righteous?

Exercise 2:

When you hear the *shofar* blowing, imagine for a moment you are on top of a mountain. You have scaled what seemed like an impossible peak. What would you name that place?

Exercise 3:

Destiny is often dependent on a series of choices. How good are you at making the decisions that will shape your destiny?

The rabbinic expression, "There is no happiness like the resolution of doubt," helps us understand that having too many choices can wear away at our happiness, keeping us in the ether of doubt and second-guessing.[5]

Choices are wonderful, but too many choices can also tyrannize. Are you a good decision-maker? A "yes" answer may help with the process of repentance. Look at the list below and circle attitudes you employ when making a decision and underline those you should make use of in the future to make change easier:

- I believe that very few decisions are irrevocable.
- I bounce ideas or questions off friends.
- I don't consult too many people. It confuses rather than clarifies.
- I name my choices and what is at stake clearly.
- I understand the possible consequences.
- I gather enough information to make an intelligent and informed decision.
- I outline every choice like a flow chart – not only the pros and cons of a decision but what might happen as a result.
- I have a strong sense of personal direction and allow decisions to flow from it.
- I work at strengthening my values and priorities to strengthen future decision-making.
- I can identify what is important and is not important about a decision.
- I have clarified my general attitude about risk-taking.
- I confront my fear of making a mistake and entertain the possibility of what a mistake might look and feel like.
- I recognize the boundaries or limitations – emotional, financial, or spiritual – of my decisions.
- I listen carefully to my gut instinct to see what it is telling me and why.
- I try not to second-guess a decision.
- I understand that sometimes there are multiple right answers, not one right answer.
- I understand that what is the right answer for someone else – even someone *like* me – may not be the right answer for me.

PASSAGES FOR ADDITIONAL STUDY

Maimonides, *Mishneh Torah, The Laws of Repentance* 3:4

Even though the sounding of the *shofar* on Rosh HaShana is a decree, it contains an allusion. It is as if [the *shofar*'s call] is saying:

Wake up you sleepy ones from your sleep and you who slumber, arise. Inspect your deeds, repent, remember your Creator. Those who forget the truth in the vanities of time and throughout the entire year, devote their energies to vanity and emptiness which will not benefit or save. Look to your souls. Improve your ways and your deeds and let every one of you abandon his evil path and thoughts.

Accordingly, throughout the entire year, a person should always look at himself as equally balanced between merit and sin, and the world as equally balanced between merit and sin. If he performs one sin, he tips his balance and that of the entire world to the side of guilt and brings destruction upon himself. [On the other hand], if he performs one mitzva, he tips his balance and that of the entire world to the side of merit and brings deliverance and salvation to himself and others.

Rabbi Moshe Haim Luzzatto, *The Path of the Just*, Chapter 6: "The Trait of Zeal"

Just as it requires great intelligence and much foresight to save oneself from the snares of the evil inclination and to escape from the evil so that it does not come to rule us and intrude itself into our deeds, so does it require great intelligence and foresight to take hold of mitzvot, to acquire them for ourselves, and not to lose them.

Rabbi Abraham Isaac Kook, *The Lights of Repentance* 2:1

Sudden repentance derives from a spiritual flash entering the soul. All at once the individual recognizes the evil and ugliness of sin and is transformed into another person. Immediately he experiences inwardly a complete change for the good. This comes about by means of a manifestation derived from an inner spiritual quality, by means of a great soulful influence whose paths merit scrutinizing to the very depths of their concealment.

Text questions to think about while studying:

- How does destiny manifest itself in these sources?
- What impact does decision-making have on the scale of righteousness?
- How does confusion get in the way of repentance?

Notes

1. To encounter this reading in greater academic depth, see Jon Levenson's seminal work, *Death and Resurrection of the Beloved Son* (New Haven: Yale University Press, 1995).
2. See James Kugel, *The God of Old* (New York: Free Press, 2004). Kugel reiterates this notion in his most recent book, *In the Valley of the Shadow* (New York: Free Press, 2011).
3. Shevuot 36a.
4. Rabbi Moshe Haim Luzzatto, *The Path of the Just* (Jerusalem: Feldheim Publishers, 1980), 48.
5. Commentary of *Metzudat David* on Proverbs 15:30.

Day Three

Discipline

"For the sin we committed before You by eating and drinking."

In the *"Al Ḥet"* sin list we read multiple times over Yom Kippur, the appearance of a confession about eating and drinking seems odd; it feels prosaic and trivial next to unwarranted hatred or speaking ill of others. It takes physical strength to fast; it takes mental determination to quell physical desire. To have that determination, you need to know what you're fasting for and why.

Tzom Gedalia, the fast of Gedalia, always follows Rosh HaShana. Most people are relieved for the break from food but do not necessarily understand why we observe this fast or what its significance is. In the annual words of my grandmother: "Who's Gedalia, anyway?" So who is Gedalia, anyway, and why is this day significant?

Gedalia was a procurator of Judah, assigned by King Nebuchadnezzar to govern the remaining Jews in Israel after the exile. Nebuchadnezzar decimated our nation and then banished the remaining residents from their land after destroying the Temple; those few who stayed became a straggling remnant of a lost nation. This is recounted in the book of II Kings: "Thus, Judah was exiled from its land. King Nebuchadnezzar of Babylon put Gedalia, son of Ahikam son of Shaphan, in charge of the people whom he left in the land of Judah" (25:21–22). There was a great deal of anxiety about the treatment of this remnant, but Gedalia reassured a group of questioning officers that if the residents stayed in the land and followed the Babylonian authorities, "It will go well with you" (25:24). Seven months later, a day which some believe was actually Rosh HaShana, Ishmael ben Nethania – one of the officers who had initially approached Gedalia and who was himself of royal descent – came with ten men and murdered Gedalia and those with him. The rest of the people left Judah for Egypt, fearing the worst.

The story is recounted in greater detail in Jeremiah 41. The day after Gedalia was killed, when no one yet knew, a group of eighty men from the area came to see him, their garments torn and their bodies gashed. They were vulnerable and beaten, but they still came bearing offerings for the Temple, gifts that would never be given. The murderer Ishmael invited them into the town to see Gedalia and then slaughtered them and threw their bodies into a cistern. Ishmael then carried any remaining stragglers off in the direction of Ammon. A warrior, Johanan ben Karea, who set out to kill Ishmael, intervened and took the rest of the people to Egypt for protection. Ishmael got away. The rabbis declared a fast day to mourn not only the death of Gedalia but the death, in many ways, of the few remaining Jews in the land of Israel, killed essentially by their own, the worst possible way to end the enduring presence of the Jews in their homeland. The destruction of even one righteous person, they believed, was the equivalent of the destruction of the House of God.[1] We fast for one – the destruction of the Temple; we must fast for the other – the destruction of a human life that represented the end of Jewish life in the land of Israel at the time. The fast is mentioned in the book of Zechariah, with the climax at the end of the verse: "You must love honesty and integrity" (8:19).

We mourn a righteous leader by fasting, but the fast is also intended to mourn the absence of Jews in the land of Israel long ago. Even when the Temple was destroyed, there was still a population of Jews inhabiting the land. After the exile, that population dwindled. But no

Jews remained in their land after the murder of Gedalia. The fast offers us the opportunity, at a time of personal reflection, to think about collective losses of identity and how often we hurt ourselves more than outsiders ever could. Ishmael's weakness made us all ultimately vulnerable.

We know the saying well. *Ethics of the Fathers* asks, "Who is strong?" and replies, "One who conquers his desires" (4:1). When we discipline ourselves to achieve our deepest goals, we have mastery over desire instead of desire having mastery over us. Acting on impulse and the momentary need for gratification can unravel our best long-term personal objectives into a moral mess that is hard to clean up. It is not easy to face the consequences of our actions, particularly of our transgressions. It takes emotional strength and resilience to face the worst of ourselves and improve our attitude and behavior without being overwhelmed by sadness or paralyzed by depression: "I just can't do it." And when we articulate those words, we really believe them. We have convinced ourselves that we have no willpower. We are weak, not strong.

Personal weaknesses so often appear on a plate. Some commentaries on the *Al Ḥet* list point to specific religious breaches connected to food. We eat without saying the appropriate blessings before and afterwards. We eat food that we shouldn't, sneaking a taste of something prohibited for a kosher-only crowd. "I'm a bad Jew," we might hear from someone who keeps kosher at home but loves a BLT on the road.

We can even get more talmudic and turn to a passage that suggests we are judged by the company we keep. A scholar, the Talmud recommends, should eat only with the wise, lest meals devolve into ribaldry and inappropriate trivialities, and lest others witness the scholar potentially compromising himself. On a similar note, *Ethics of the Fathers* advises that every meal involving three people be accompanied by a teaching moment to sanctify the food, a *dvar Torah*. We may confess on Yom Kippur for failing to make an ordinary meal into a time of shared study; we rushed a Shabbat meal to get a nap and did not sanctify that meal by sharing Torah. For that we confess.

And yet, despite all of the potential spiritual infractions possibly hinted at in this confession, there is another larger and looming question: am I eating and drinking the way that I should, the way that optimizes my health and minimizes any addictions or bad habits born of years of socialized behavior? We adopt food-related behaviors very early and may spend a lifetime fighting them or resigning ourselves to them but never quite relinquishing the residual emotional impact that this tension presents. Food is rarely an emotionally neutral subject, and when we speak about it in a prayer for self-improvement we understand that it is part of a larger conversation about self-discipline and achieving objectives incrementally, objectives that must be secured and maintained day after day after day.

We are what we eat. We are how we eat. We are the way we manage everyday behavior that can easily spiral out of control, breaking the biblical prohibition: "But take utmost care and watch yourselves scrupulously" (Deuteronomy 4:9). We are commanded by God to take the utmost care of the body that houses the soul. Maimonides writes that when the body suffers, the soul cannot achieve its great heights. Sickness is consumptive; it eats time and distracts us from focusing on other matters. Our faith demands that health must be of supreme personal concern, and one of the markers of good health is food consumption or restraint.

It is easy enough to imagine cases of transgression that seem deserving of a confession. It's the obese young man with the growing waistline who tells his doctor he is dieting but is secretly hiding stashes of junk food all around the house. It's the thin high school senior battling anorexia who looks in the mirror and sees someone ugly and heavy before her. It's the middle-aged woman in a failing marriage who has a drinking problem, but denies it to her friends and children who desperately want her to get help. It's the grandfather with diabetes who keeps plying his grandchildren with candy and always orders cake in restaurants.

But why only look at the extreme cases when ordinary living poses so many daily food challenges? Betraying the simple goals we set for ourselves that keep us in good health is also worthy of a few lines of reflection once a year, so we say the confession along with everyone else. I keep Philo of Alexandria's quote in my wallet: "Be kind, for everyone you meet is fighting a great battle." Great is in the eye of the beholder.

New York Times restaurant critic Frank Bruni wrote a memoir of his lifelong struggle with food, *Born Round: The Secret History of a Full-Time Eater.* The picture on the book's back cover shows a svelte journalist who seems, on the surface, to be winning the battle. In this memoir he talks about his own food lies, the lies he told himself about his metabolism and habits and the lies he told others about what he was eating and drinking. This surfaced for him in a particularly ironic way when he was asked to transition from political correspondent to restaurant critic, which meant getting paid to eat. He describes the insanity of the decision to plunge into a world of constant eating when he had struggled with his weight constantly. Bruni finally concludes that what had changed most about him when his weight was under control "wasn't determination. It was honesty." He stopped lying to himself about the damage food could and did do and knew that his body was speaking to him with all the warning signs. He just chose to ignore them. "The care and the candor are the challenge," he says, and "one botched day or even one botched week wasn't apocalyptic. It was life as most people lived it – certainly as I did."[2]

The tug-of-war of food and self-discipline begins early in Jewish texts. We find an odd swath of talmudic discourse in chapter eight of Yoma, which focuses on repentance, specifically on Yom Kippur and its prohibitions. Because we are fasting, we often think about food and our relationship to it even more than usual. Into these debates enters a disquisition on repentance and the biblical transitional food of our wilderness trek to the Promised Land: manna. Manna was a strange food, introduced in Exodus 16 when the Israelites were starving and protested that Moses and Aaron had not made sufficient accommodation for their hunger in the desert. God gave them food, but it was not at all what they had in mind:

> In the morning there was a fall of dew about the camp. When the fall of dew lifted, there, over the surface of the wilderness, lay a fine and flaky substance, as fine as frost on the ground. When the Israelites saw it, they said to one another, "What is it?" – for they did not know what it was. And Moses said to them, "This is the bread which the Lord has given you to eat." (Exodus 16:13–15)

Manna is actually named for the experience of confusion, shifting the language slightly from "*Man hu*?" – what is it? – to manna. They named the food after a question. This was faith food, soul food, and they had no prior acquaintance with it. But for the next forty years, until the early chapters of Joshua, this was virtually the only food they would know. When they entered the land, the day after they offered the Passover sacrifice, the manna stopped its heavenly descent: "On that same day, when they ate of the produce of the land, the manna ceased. The Israelites got no more manna; that year they ate of the yield of the land of Canaan" (Joshua 5:12).

The manna was designed as a spiritual food to test the Israelites' faith. This was stated from the outset: "I will rain down bread for you from the sky, and the people shall go out and gather each day that day's portion – *that I may test them, to see whether they will follow My instructions or not*" (Exodus 16:4). Food can become a test in a Pavlovian sense. If you observe certain conditions, then you will receive your due. But it seems that God had something different in mind because the food itself was special; it was divinely produced and distributed. The fact that God created an essentially different food for the journey puzzled the rabbis of the Talmud, who waxed eloquently on the manna's properties specifically as a food of repentance. It not only fueled the Israelites physically, it strengthened them internally, to help them transition out of their slavish dependence on masters for sustenance and accustom themselves to One Master who provided for them but also forced them to partner in food gathering and preparation. Helping the Israelites adjust to an autonomous lifestyle in a homeland would require an inherent shift of behavior and attitude. The manna was there as a faith tool.

The manna was round and white and was delivered on dew throughout the camp: "The people would go about and gather it, grind it between millstones or pound it in a mortar, boil it in a pot, and make it into cakes" (Numbers 11:8). The sages analyzed manna's penitential properties through verses like this and used playful word dissections to discover what about it promoted faith. They concluded that manna was white because "it makes white [cleanses] the sins of Israel."[3] It had the capacity to make people vulnerable and open, revealing truths that might otherwise have been hidden. One sage wondered why the manna was delivered daily and not annually, answering that the daily distribution stimulated the Israelites to consider every day whether they were worthy of divine food. An annual gift would not have secured this kind of instant and constant attentiveness to their relationship with God or to their own behavior: "Thus they were found to turn their attention to their Father in heaven."[4] The various verbs suggesting different ways the manna was distributed and cooked were understood by the sages as a public statement of goodness. If you were righteous, the manna was delivered to your tent door already in the form of bread. If you were wicked, you had to travel to get it and then pound it with a mortar to make it into flour. If you were neither righteous nor wicked, the manna had to be gathered but was not far away and appeared as cakes. Manna was the food of faith because the food was a visible, public witness to your behavior. It stood in judgment of your deeds through its daily delivery.

The Israelites were mid-trek when they struggled mightily with temptation and suffered food fatigue. They were tired of the manna and its blandness: "Now our gullets are shriveled. There is nothing at all! Nothing but this manna to look at!" (Numbers 11:6). One medieval exegete described their gullets as dry and parched as a result of this heaven-sent bread.[5] In other words, they lost sight of its heavenly properties and only experienced its limitations. They were desperate for meat and wanted to know if this God of theirs could provide them with the near impossible in the wilderness: a glut of meat. The text proceeds to tell us with visual insight what the Israelites suddenly experienced in response to their food cravings, rich in sensual detail:

> A wind from the Lord started up, swept quail from the sea and strewed them over the camp, about a day's journey on this side and about a day's journey on that side, and some two cubits deep on the ground. The people set to gathering quail all day and night and all the next day…and they spread them out all around the camp. The meat was still between their teeth, nor yet chewed, when the anger of the Lord blazed forth against the people and the Lord struck the people with a very severe plague. That place was named Kibroth-hattaava because the people who had the craving were buried there. (Numbers 11:31–34)

Unlike the manna that was delivered on divine dew at a set time, the text emphasizes the collapse of time. The people in their greed ate day and night, without restraint. They saw meat everywhere they looked, piled high and dense. They traveled a day's journey to get it, and when they saw it, they ravaged the quail flesh. The image of a plague striking them while the meat was still between their teeth, not yet chewed into food but stuffed into their formerly parched gullets, is graphic and revolting. We have little sympathy for these whining, excessive Israelites whose taste buds were more important than God's larger vision, which required patience and discipline. The place name given for this incident literally means "graves of desire." Desire can become a tombstone, a marker of everything that we fail to do to preserve our best instincts and desires.

Today, we know more about willpower and its limitations than we ever have. Psychologist Roy Baumeister and journalist John Tierney, in their book *Willpower,* state the belief that willpower alone is our greatest human strength.[6] In an earlier book by Baumeister, he and his co-authors concluded that "self-regulation failure is the major social pathology of our time," relating it to increases in crime, divorce, and domestic violence.[7]

At the same time, Baumeister believes, willpower needs resistance training. You can develop more willpower if you use your willpower. The downside is that, like a muscle, willpower also gets depleted with fatigue and overuse. Kelly McGonigal, in *The Willpower Instinct,* believes that willpower is not a mind-over-body response but an actual biological function that is adaptive with proper nurturing. Too much self-control can have negative effects, just as temptation and stress can place an unnecessary burden on the willpower muscle. Practice helps us make progress. In fact, Tierney praises observant religious people, believing that they are a good example of how self-discipline shapes character and builds self-control.

In a radio interview, Tierney said, "Just putting food where you can see it next to you depletes your willpower. Whereas putting it away in a drawer or putting it across the room makes it easier for you because you're not actively resisting the temptation."[8] Tierney also warned about being careful with willpower since one has only a finite amount of it: "conserve it and try to save it for the emergencies."

Psychological tests done on students have borne this out. Those who resisted the temptation to eat cookies, for example, did more poorly on tests later in the day since they required more self-discipline overall. Holding back desire for a significant period of time can result in a binge release. The message: pick what you need to be disciplined about because it is impossible to have the mental strength to overcome all desire. Researchers refer to usage of finite willpower as "ego depletion." In fact, McGonigal believes that when our discipline fails and we beat ourselves up over it with guilt and shame, we may be lessening the chances for willpower to kick in in the future. Those with self-compassion and self-forgiveness generally also have the best self-control.

McGonigal argues that often when it comes to thinking about and changing ourselves, there is a disconnect between our current behavior and attitudes and the way that we imagine ourselves to be in some unknown future. In that future, we imagine that we will behave differently than we do now. We will be nicer, slimmer, more generous, and more carefree. Perhaps our future Jewish selves will learn more, give more *tzedaka,* and pray with more consistency and intention. But McGonigal believes that it is much more likely that the future looks a lot like our present when it comes to the self. Psychological tests reveal that when people saw digitally age-enhanced versions of themselves and then were given a thousand dollars, they allocated double the money to their retirement fund. Students who were given a choice of volunteering this semester or next were willing to give twenty-seven minutes to doing good this semester; those signing up the for the following semester volunteered eighty-five minutes. When asked to volunteer others, students signed up peers for 120 minutes.[9] We demand more of our future selves and others than we demand of ourselves now. Why? Because we envision that we will be better tomorrow than we are today.

But a wish is not the same thing as the kind of behavior management that would brush away our doubts and actually set us on a real course for improvement in the days ahead. Every Yom Kippur we imagine a tomorrow filled with piety, until we actually get there and discover that too often, without a plan in place, the week after Yom Kippur looks a lot like the week before it.

And even though they say that bad habits are hard to break, Charles Duhigg, in his recent book, *The Power of Habit,* argues that the more we know about how we form our habits, the easier they are to change. He amasses scientific evidence to show that difficult tasks repeated multiple times become rote. We may barely think about what we do when we shoot a basket, drive a car, or take a shower because we go into automatic pilot. We've done things so many times that our bodies engage even if our minds are coasting. David Brooks, writing on Duhigg, claims that "your willpower is not like a dam that can block the torrent of self-indulgence. It's more like a muscle, which tires easily."[10] It needs to be fortified.

If repetition is the key to habit, then recalibrating behaviors and performing them differently, again and again, becomes one critical way that we break bad habits and willfully choose new ones. When we learn new routines and practice them repeatedly, we "teach" ourselves to adopt the best practices. It is awkward at first but still doable. Research conducted at Duke University shows that 40 percent of our behaviors are formed through habit rather than intentional decisions. With a little concerted mental effort, we can reshape old habits.[11] We can train ourselves to follow new habits to the extent that they become a permanent fixture of the way we operate in any given realm, repeating new behaviors until they have the ease of old habits. Habits are like friends; it takes a long time to make a new friend an old friend. It is common to underestimate how long the integration of these new habits will take.

The research on willpower corresponds with much of what we read in *Musar* literature, ethical works largely developed in nineteenth-century Eastern and Western Europe to aid in spiritual growth and self-improvement. The world of *Musar* presents the forces of good and evil – *yetzer hatov* and *yetzer hara* – in constant battle with each other. We are the battlefield where the fighting takes place. Rabbi Eliyahu Dessler (1892–1953), in one of the most important works of *Musar, Strive for Truth,* makes the battlefield a place of small victories and large obstacles.

Rabbi Dessler was the scion of a rabbinic family and the founder of the Gateshead Yeshiva in the north of England. In 1947, he moved to Bnei Brak to learn and teach in Israel. Notes taken by his students during his lectures formed the basis of *Strive for Truth,* a book prepared by one of his disciples, Aryeh Carmell. One of Rabbi Dessler's most noted contributions to the world of Jewish self-improvement lies in his observations on the *beḥira* point.[12] *Beḥira* is the Hebrew term for "choice," but specifically refers to choices made of one's free will. Rabbi Dessler compared our moral choices to life on the battlefield. He writes, "When two armies are locked in battle, fighting takes place only at the battlefront."[13] Any territory behind the lines of either army is assumed to be in the possession of that army. If one army pushes the other back, then that territory, too, becomes the assumed possession of that particular army. He compares this notion of the point where the troops meet to choices that individuals make:

> The situation is very similar with regard to *beḥira*. Everyone has free choice – at the point where truth meets falsehood. In other words, *beḥira* takes place at the point where the truth as the person sees it confronts the illusion produced in him by the power of falsehood. But the majority of a person's actions are undertaken without any clash between truth and falsehood taking place.[14]

Most decisions we make, Rabbi Dessler argues, are not a struggle for us. We may have been raised with certain values that operate within us naturally. For example, a person raised within a framework of *kashrut* observance will not think twice about whether or not to eat something non-kosher, thus the popular salami diet. A person who keeps kosher may fight the urge for chocolate but may never fight the temptation for ham. If he pops a piece of salami in his mouth in the presence of milk chocolate, cheese cake, or a milkshake, chances are good that he will have no desire to eat dairy products (because of the lengthy separation between milk and meat for kosher-only eaters). There is no struggle for that individual; therefore, the *beḥira* point is not activated. In addition, Rabbi Dessler believes that "any behavior a person adopts as a result of training or by copying others is not counted as his own,"[15] since this is not his own battlefield. He cannot praise himself for not eating ham. He can only praise himself for exercising discipline to overcome a challenge that he actually has. In Rabbi Dessler's words, "*Beḥira* comes into play only when one is tempted to go against the truth as one sees it and the forces on either side are more or less equally balanced."[16] We want to move from desire to clarity. "The ultimate aim of all of our service is to graduate from freedom to compulsion. We do not want to remain in that confused state in which 'truth' and 'falsehood' seem equally valid alternatives."[17]

The moral battlefield is one that we create and one that we largely control. While we cannot control what we are up against, we do control how we respond to it. When we battle the forces against us and make good choices, we can get to the point that Rabbi Dessler calls compulsion. We feel utterly compelled to make good decisions; we have so profoundly integrated good choices that it would not occur to us to make poor ones. Thus, we have changed the battlefield. In order to change it, we have to spend time discovering our *beḥira* point.

Imagine a person who battles every day with a weight problem. Every time he or she takes food, the battle rages within. After extensive dieting and overcoming recurring health problems, this individual no longer faces the same battlefield because he or she has integrated more healthful eating habits. Rabbi Dessler calls this "higher unfreedom."

There is an even higher level on the battleground. Compulsion is still an active force, a decision, even if it is a decision for good. At a certain point of commitment, individuals do good for the sake of goodness; there is no compulsion at all. Doing right is simply natural. "Compulsion applies only where there is resistance. One cannot speak of compulsion to do something one loves."[18]

Rabbi Dessler helps us consider the humanity of the moral struggle and our place within it. The point of choice on a battleground is the place where equally compelling forces are pulling us in different directions and where an active choice is required. The more our capacity to do good becomes instinctive, the more able we are to move the lines on the battlefield so that we possess more moral territory. For those who are able with constancy and regularity to conquer the forces working against them through active choice, freedom turns into compulsion. That compulsion turns into love. At that point, the individual has achieved Rabbi Dessler's goal: "The man of the spirit is the truly liberated man."

A liberated person is one who engages his or her self-control at will. Self-control is the ultimate strength. We can fight the battle within and win. The past is not something we can control. But with our own willpower in place, we can redeem it in the future.

Sadly, we cannot change past failures. Looking back on a stained history, we wonder what would have happened had Ishmael not murdered Gedalia and others on that fateful day. What would have happened had Ishmael had more self-control? We may have rebuilt our community in Israel out of the ashes of destruction, as we have done successfully so many times since. But we will never know. Weakness prevailed. We can only defeat it looking forward and redeem gratuitous hatred with overpowering love.

LIFE HOMEWORK

Task 1: Name one of your *beḥira* points. Take a moment to write down three areas where self-control is easy for you and then three where it is not. Try to draw a map of your personal battlefield. Place your soldiers – your willpower muscle – where they need to be to fight from your place of strength. When you can visualize that place, it will be easier to move forward with your goals, identifying the obstacles without letting them derail you. Beware of ego depletion, so use willpower where you need it most because it does run out. And while you are working from your strengths, try to leverage this fast day caused by baseless hatred with one small act of inexplicable love.

The Hasidic Rebbe, Mordechai of Lekhovitz, once attended the *brit*, the circumcision, of a friend's son. The rebbe was presented with the baby for a blessing. The blessing was simple: "May you not fool God, may you not fool yourself, and may you not fool people."[19] In other words, don't be a hypocrite. Be true and transparent so that you can own up to weakness. Be honest with yourself and you will be honest with others.

Task 2: Name a food challenge. Do not judge it initially. Simply name it. Write the challenge down on a piece of paper. Beneath it, add other aspects that this problem brings to light.

Food challenge:

- How is this really a character challenge?
- What are the consequences of this challenge?
- How honest are you about this challenge?
- What will be the lasting outcome of overcoming this challenge?

Naming this problem and its attendant consequences makes this challenge more real. What will you do about it now that you have confessed it? How will you use your confession on Yom Kippur about eating and drinking as the start of better habits?

PASSAGES FOR ADDITIONAL STUDY

Maimonides, *Mishneh Torah, The Laws of Repentance* 2:1

[Who has reached] complete teshuva? A person who confronts the same situation in which he sinned when he has the potential to commit [the sin again], and, nevertheless, abstains and does not commit it because of his teshuva alone and not because of fear or a lack of strength. For example, a person engaged in illicit sexual relations with a woman. Afterwards, they met in privacy, in the same country, while his love for her and physical power still persisted, and nevertheless, he abstained and did not transgress. This is a complete Baal-teshuva [penitent].... If he does not repent until his old age, at a time when he is incapable of doing what he did before, even though this is not a high level of repentance, he is a Baal-teshuva. Even if he transgressed throughout his entire life and repented on the day of his death and died in repentance, all his sins are forgiven...

Rabbi Moshe Haim Luzzatto, *The Path of the Just*, Chapter 1: "Concerning Man's Duty in the World"

The Holy One Blessed Be He has put man in a place where the factors which draw him further from the Blessed One are many. There are the earthly desires, which, if he is pulled after them, cause him to be drawn further from and to depart from the true good. It is seen, then, that man is veritably placed in the midst of a raging battle.

Rabbi Abraham Isaac Kook, *The Lights of Repentance* 7:4

The thought of repentance is that which reveals the depth of will, and the strength of the soul is revealed by means of these thoughts in the fullness of its splendor; in accordance with the extent of repentance, so is the degree of the soul's freedom.

Text questions to think about while studying:

- How does heightened discipline help us achieve repentance?
- What factors pull us away from the true good?
- How is discipline related to the "soul's freedom"?

Notes

1. Rosh HaShana 18b.
2. Frank Bruni, *Born Round: The Secret History of a Full-Time Eater* (New York: Penguin Press, 2009), 248.
3. Berakhot 75a.
4. Ibid., 76a.
5. See the comments of Rashbam, Rabbi Samuel ben Meir, on this verse.
6. Roy Baumeister and John Tierney, *Willpower* (New York: Penguin, 2011); see also Kelly McGonigal, *The Willpower Instinct* (New York: Avery, 2011).
7. See Roy Baumeister, Dianne Tice, and Todd Heatherton, *Losing Control* (San Diego: Academic Press, 1994).
8. See National Public Radio, "Resistance Training for Your 'Willpower' Muscles," http://www.npr.org/2011/09/18/140516974/resistance-training-for-your-willpower-muscles.
9. See the work of psychology professor Emily Pronin of Princeton University as cited in Alina Tugend, "Bad Habits? My Future Self Will Deal with That," *New York Times*, February 25, 2012, B5.
10. David Brooks, "The Machiavellian Impulse," *New York Times*, March 1, 2012, http://www.nytimes.com/2012/03/02/opinion/brooks-the-machiavellian-temptation.html?_r=1.
11. See Charles Duhigg, *The Power of Habit* (New York: Random House, 2012) and a review of it, "Can't Help Myself," by Timothy D. Wilson, *New York Times Book Review*, March 11, 2012, 15.
12. Rabbi Eliyahu Dessler, *Strive for Truth*, trans. Aryeh Carmell (Jerusalem: Feldheim Publishers, 2004); see parts 1–4 in the three-volume set. The *beḥira* point appears throughout Rabbi Dessler's book and in collected sermons.
13. Ibid., 52.
14. Ibid., 53.
15. Ibid., 60.
16. Ibid., 54.
17. Ibid., 62.
18. Ibid., 62–63.
19. Martin Buber, *Tales of the Hasidim: Later Masters* (New York: Schocken Books, 1977), 155.

Day Four

Humility

"For the sin we committed before You by haughtily stretching forth the neck."

The word humility is rooted in the Latin word for "grounded" or "low," from the word "humus" or earth. To be a person of the earth is to realize that one is small. We come from the earth and will return to it, in Job's immortal words; while we occupy it, we should take up a smaller spiritual footprint to make space for others. To be humble is to think modestly of one's abilities and one's place in the world. Being humble also means that we have the emotional bandwidth to make others feel good about themselves without believing that it detracts from our own sense of security. Humble people have the capacity to honor others. Arrogant people hoard all credit for themselves – as if complimenting others detracts from oneself.

A young man on the rise in his company shared his distress with me. One of his close colleagues, a man in a senior position, confessed to him out of the office when his guard was down that he hated hearing about his younger colleague's successes. It frustrated him to no end that this rising star was sucking away attention from others, mostly from himself. He resented this man's talent and was openly jealous. When we spoke about it, he was unsure what to do. Working hard was not enough. He had to learn to work hard and not have anyone notice, since his success was taking away from the success of his superiors.

Elie Wiesel famously said that one of the lessons he learned from receiving the Nobel Peace Prize was who his friends were. They were the people who could feel genuine happiness for his success, not begrudge him out of envy or spite. A test of true friendship and support is not only whether others empathize with our travails, but also whether they are able to rejoice in our better moments and compliment freely and sincerely. Friends celebrate the success of others, as it states in *Ethics of the Fathers*, "Let your friend's honor be as dear to you as your own" (2:10). The capacity to honor and recognize the goodness and achievement of others is a signature of personal humility and security. If it is hard to compliment others, to make others feel good, then we have to look in the mirror and ask ourselves why.

Humility is critical to the life of the spirit because it enables us to accept a subordinate position in relation to others and God. If we take up every word in a dialogue it becomes a soliloquy. If we take up all the space in a room, there is no room for God.

We stretch forth our necks in sin when we allow ourselves to sit in judgment over others. By making someone else inferior, we become more superior in our own eyes. Our necks metaphorically extend higher and then look down at others. Rabbi Luzzatto wrote about humility and arrogance throughout the pages of *The Path of the Just*, understanding that this battle preoccupies us all. It is a constant fight within.

> Pride consists in a person's pluming himself with his self and considering himself worthy of praise. There can be many different reasons behind this. Some deem themselves intelligent; some, handsome; some, honored; some, great; some, wise.... When a man attributes to himself any of the good things of the world, he puts himself in immediate danger of falling into the pit of pride.[1]

The pit of pride can swallow us whole. Rabbi Luzzatto believed that arrogance alone "stultifies the mind, which perverts the hearts of the highest in wisdom."[2]

Rabbi Moshe Teitelbaum (1759–1841), the Rebbe of Ujhely, Hungary, and a convert to Hasidut through his son-in-law, told this story in notes he made on the dreams of his youth. It is a good example of the pit of pride we must avoid. Rabbi Teitelbaum was looking out his window on the night of Rosh HaShana and watched as a throng of people hurried to the synagogue: "I saw that they were driven by the fear of the Day of Judgment." He watched this with an outstretched neck and said to himself: "God be thanked, I have been doing the right thing all through the year! I have studied right and prayed right, so I do not have to be afraid." Watching the sudden rush to synagogue did not stir panic within him. His good deeds and character were all in check. Why hurry? With this confidence he examined his dreams to review all his good works. "I looked and looked: They were torn, ragged, ruined! At that instant I woke up. Overcome with fear, I ran to the House of Prayer along with the rest."[3]

We recognize Rabbi Moshe's stability. It is the posture of an overconfident man entering the Day of Judgment. We have all been there. Rosh HaShana catches us by surprise. We are blessedly unprepared. We feel good about ourselves. And why shouldn't we? But then we pause to think more deeply about the year past and our regrets and mistakes, and suddenly we are overcome with Rabbi Moshe's panic. Humility gets the better of us. Get thee to a synagogue. Fast.

In the synagogue at this time of year, we take ourselves out of the pit of pride and throw ourselves willingly into the pit of humility. Our prayers are designed to help us acknowledge our smallness in the universe. One of the most famous of these is an evening *piyut*, an acrostic poem of anonymous authorship, sung during *Kol Nidrei*:

> Like the clay in the hand of a potter
> Who thickens or thins it at his will,
> So are we in Thy hand, gracious God,
> Forgive our sin, Thy covenant fulfill.

> Like a stone in the hand of the mason
> Who preserves or breaks it at his will,
> So are we in Thy hand, Lord of life,
> Forgive our sin, Thy covenant fulfill.
>
> Like iron in the hand of the craftsman
> Who forges or cools it at his will,
> We are in Thy hand, our Keeper,
> Forgive our sin, Thy covenant fulfill.[4]

The request for forgiveness stays the same, but the way we refer to ourselves and to God changes. We review the different ways that God relates to us with mercy and authority, giving us life and sustaining us, as would a craftsman. We are mere raw material. Any ingredient of uniqueness we may possess – our health, our wealth, good looks, or a good mind – is God's doing and in God's hands to mold. It has little to do with us.

But even as we raise our voices in song and lower our impulse of pride, we know the synagogue is also no safe place to escape the ego, especially during the Days of Awe. People are interested in ladies' hats and suits and expensive jewelry. People are interested in who sits in what row. People are interested in others who sway and bow, the piety of those they observe in their peripheral vision. People are interested in the food served in various homes at festive meals after services. The fear and reverence that should comprise our awe is often compromised by our curiosity over the material or perceived spiritual excesses in our midst.

Rabbi Joseph Telushkin tells a story of his grandfather, also a rabbi. His grandfather served in the rabbinate for sixty years and told his grandson about a certain wealthy man in his congregation who was entitled to sit in a prime seat in the front of the congregation. He, instead, chose to sit in the back, watching others enter the sanctuary to see if they would notice that he was not sitting in the front. The elder Rabbi Telushkin finally confronted the wealthy man: "It would be better if you sat up front, and thought you should be seated in the back, rather than to sit in the back, and think the whole time you should be seated in the front."[5]

Sometimes we inherit the success of others, which we deem a cause for superiority: status, family wealth, or position in the community.

Sometimes we work really hard to achieve material or academic success, and it happens, bloating us with pride. The sages of the Talmud pondered the question of why many Torah scholars have children who are not Torah scholars. Many of their answers have to do with arrogance. A scholar who regards himself as superior to others might make a child question whether religion matters. The child then opts out of religion.[6]

Even in the arena of Torah study, a cardinal value of Jewish life, scholarship is riddled with battles for status. This problem was addressed outright in *Ethics of the Fathers*: "Do not give yourself airs if you have learned much Torah, because it is for this purpose you were created" (2:8). We are entitled to feel joy when we have discovered and are living our life's purpose, but joy is not the same as superiority. Superiority only brings down the spirit and ruins the reputation of the mind as a tool for meaning. It too often becomes a tool for status, even – and some could argue especially – among Torah scholars.

There is little in the world more insufferable than self-righteousness. Those who suffer from it believe that God is on their side, supporting the piety of the observant against the ignorance of those who are not. Self-righteousness lies at the very heart of the fundamentalist, making him police officer, judge, and prosecutor. In contrast, God makes a small request through the agency of the prophet. "Act justly, love mercy, and walk humbly with your God" (Micah 6:8). Micah asks this of us as if it were easy and imposed no great burden. Yet the burden of humility is the very fact that we have to remind ourselves of it always.

Humility can be a result of the way we were raised, a character trait we come by easily – or it may have been conditioned by a change of circumstances. Tragic experiences often take a person from a place of pride to a place of humility. The person who stretches forth his neck above others becomes the very same person who sits with his head bowed because life suddenly took an unexpected turn for the worse. When all is well, we give ourselves extra credit, believing that we are worthy of all of our successes. But when a change of fortune sets in, it is not only that we lose something concrete – like a spouse or a job or our savings – but we also lose a self-image consonant with success. The captain-of-the-universe posture rusts into a confusing, beguiling, and disappointing mess.

Just ask Job. There is no better story to illustrate this than the spiritual whiplash suffered by Job. Job had everything: a large family, wealth, and status born of his wisdom. And then Job became the unwitting victim in a wager between God and Satan: God believed that a faithful servant would be loyal in any circumstance; Satan believed that only those who are blessed stay true to God. God pointed to the person He deemed most successful in the ancient Near East: Job of the land of Uz. Job is introduced as a man who was "blameless and upright; he feared God and shunned evil" (Job 1:1). He had ten children – seven of whom were boys, a sure sign of blessing in the days of old – and a vast estate. "The man was wealthier than anyone in the East" (1:3). But by the end of the first chapter, Job had lost all of his children, and his world quickly unraveled.

Later in the story, Job reflects on the man he had once been in his prime: "O that I were as in months gone by, in the days when God watched over me, when His lamp shone over my head, when I walked in the dark by His light" (29:2). At that time, Job says, his children surrounded him and his feet "were bathed in cream" (29:6). He had the attention of nobles; young men hid from him out of fear. He helped others who were unfortunate; men would listen for his words of wisdom. He describes his words as drops of dew to men who were thirsty for his counsel. But after calamity struck, he walked in the streets ashamed and denigrated, a man of little worth among friends.

It must have felt good to be regarded so highly, to walk into a room and have people hang on your every word and enjoy "love like a king among his troops, like one who consoles mourners" (29:25). The one who consoles mourners extends pity to others; he never imagines himself as an object of pity to others.

In the very first chapters that follow his catalogue of woes, Job begins to understand his altered position and curses his very existence: "Perish the day on which I was born and the night it was announced.... May that day be darkness. May God have no concern for it. May light not shine upon it" (3:4–5). Job never curses God; he only wonders at why he was ever brought into existence. The worst tragedy that could befall him struck. The nightmare of all nightmares was real:

> My groaning serves as my bread;
> My roaring pours forth as water.
> For what I feared has overtaken me;
> What I dreaded has come upon me.
> I had no repose, no quiet, no rest.
> And trouble came. (3:24–26)

A man of prominence stops eating. A mouth that once could afford any delicacy is filled with groaning. His most dreaded fears have come true, leaving him without any respite. And what happens in the over forty chapters that follow is the total transformation of a man of success into a brittle version of his former self. His faith stays constant, but his pride is replaced with despondency.

The secret of Job's humility was no secret at all. As his life shrunk in its capacity for blessing, Job questioned all of the assumptions that lead to success, particularly the belief in human mastery. The mortal hubris of achievement was crushed in a single blow, leaving Job winded.

As the book nears its end, God speaks directly to Job, asking Job if he has an inkling of understanding of how the world works. God moves Job's ruminations from self-pity by asking him to contemplate the complexity of a world far beyond his comprehension:

> Where were you when I laid the earth's foundations?
> Speak if you have understanding.
> Do you know who fixed its dimensions
> Or who measured it with a line?
> Onto what were its bases sunk?
> Who set its cornerstone
> When the morning stars sang together
> And all the divine beings shouted for joy? (38:4–7)

God, the divine structural engineer, questions Job about the foundations of the universe and who set it all in motion. As if Job's tragedies had not humbled him sufficiently, God in the next several chapters continues to question Job about seemingly every facet of the world: lightning, the ocean, clouds, snow, constellations, the hunting instinct of the lion, the season when mountain goats give birth, the way an ostrich beats its wings, the way the eagle soars. All of nature is governed by a force so vast that no person, however wise, can conceive of it all. We read Job and are reminded of the poem "Design," in which Robert Frost meditates on "a dimpled spider, fat and white." He looks at it closely and marvels at its intricacies and its capacity to frighten human beings:

> What but design of darkness to appall?–
> If design govern in a thing so small.

God asks Job if he can possibly understand the natural world, the design of each creature and its relationship to the ecosystem that God manufactured. To this, Job can muster only silence and a weak response, the response of humility:

> See, I am of small worth. What can I answer You? I clap my hands to my mouth. (40:4)

We, too, are small in God's immense universe. Practice humility. Making ourselves smaller helps us appreciate the vastness of a world so much larger than we are.

LIFE HOMEWORK

Task 1: Imagine for a moment that you are being honored or are receiving an award. Identify what you might be honored for at this moment. A friend of mine sets his professional achievement goals this way: he imagines what he would want to be honored for five years from now and works towards it. Think about what it would be like to stand in front of a podium and be recognized for that achievement.

Now imagine that there is no certificate, no award, no crystal plaque with your name on it. The award you will get instead has nothing to do with your profession or your academic achievements. It is awarded by your children or your parents or a friend because you set as your goal the honor and needs of someone else. We get that award long from now in the eulogies that one day will be offered when we are no longer around to hear them. What would you like someone to say about you at your funeral?

Task 2: Think of someone in your life who is not expecting to hear from you and who has just achieved something of importance. Go out of your way to celebrate his or her success in detail, letting him or her know how proud you are and why. In the spirit of *Ethics of the Fathers,* let your friend's honor be as dear to you as your own.

PASSAGES FOR ADDITIONAL STUDY

Maimonides, *Mishneh Torah, The Laws of Repentance* 4:2

Five deeds cause the paths of teshuva to be locked before those who commit them. They are: a) One who separates himself from the community – When they repent, he will not be together with them and he will not merit to share in their merit. b) One who contradicts the words of the Sages – The controversy he provokes will cause him to cut himself off from them and, thus, he will never know the ways of repentance. c) One who scoffs at the mitzvot – Since he considers them as degrading, he will not pursue them or fulfill them. If he does not fulfill mitzvot, how can he merit [to repent]? d) One who demeans his teachers –

This will cause them to reject and dismiss him.... In this period of rejection, he will not find a teacher or guide to show him the path of truth. e) One who hates admonishment – This will not leave him a path for repentance. Admonishment leads to teshuva. When a person is informed about his sins and shamed because of them, he will repent...

Rabbi Moshe Haim Luzzatto, *The Path of the Just*, Chapter 22: "The Trait of Humility"

Unquestionably, humility removes many stumbling blocks from a man's path and brings him nearer to many good things; for the Humble man is little concerned with worldly affairs and is not moved to envy by its vanities. Furthermore, his company is very pleasant and he gives pleasure to his fellowmen. He is perforce never aroused to anger and to controversy; he does everything quietly and calmly. Happy are those who are privileged to acquire this trait!

Rabbi Abraham Isaac Kook, *The Lights of Repentance*, Introduction

My inner being impels me to speak about penitence, but I recoil inwardly from my intention. Am I worthy to discuss the subject of penitence? The greatest spirits of past generations wrote on the subject of penitence, including the prophets, the noblest of sages, the greatest of the saints, and how dare I place myself in their category? But no reticence can relieve me of this inner claim. I must speak about penitence, particularly about its literary and practical aspects, to understand its significance for our generation, and the manner of its implementation in life, the life of the individual and the life of society.

Text questions to think about while studying:

- How is humility related to accepting feedback?
- Why does the humble person bring pleasure to others?
- How can you balance your reverence for the wisdom of others with the expression of your own originality?

Notes

1. Rabbi Moshe Haim Luzzatto, *The Path of the Just* (Jerusalem: Feldheim Publishers, 1980), 155.
2. Ibid., 159.
3. Martin Buber, *Tales of the Hasidim: Later Masters* (New York: Schocken Books, 1977), 189.
4. Translated by Ben Zion Bokser in *The High Holiday Prayer Book* (New York: Hebrew Publishing Co., 1959), 285.
5. Joseph Telushkin, *Jewish Wisdom* (New York: William Morrow, 1994), 226.
6. See Nedarim 81a.

Day Five

Compassion

> *"We have turned away from Your commandments and from Your redeeming laws, and we have gained nothing from it."*

Jonah has been depicted in ancient floor mosaics and on the ceiling of the Sistine Chapel. He is a figure of interest in the three major Western faiths, and scholars have been piqued for centuries by this strange aquatic tale. The book bearing his name is one of the shortest in the Bible, and the only one that ends with a question. Its pages depict the defiance of a prophet, Jonah's resignation to accept a mission, and his eventual failure to carry through the task. In Christian polemics, Jonah is regarded as a disturbed Hebrew prophet who pales in religious commitment to the sailors and citizens of Nineveh, all of whom seem more contrite than one of God's anointed. It is reported in a Hadith that Muhammad once said, "One should not say that I am better than Jonah, son of Amitai."

This negativity shows a lack of insight into the true struggle in the book: the battle between justice and compassion. On one level, Jonah turns away from God's command, gains nothing, and loses everything, just like the confession we read every Yom Kippur: "We have turned away from Your commandments and from Your redeeming laws and we have gained nothing from it." Virtually all of the sins that follow are a result of a deeper chasm; we have turned away from God and our lives begin to fall apart. But on another level, Jonah runs away because, in his stark and rigid view of good and evil, he has little room for compassion for others but demands it for himself. His is a struggle that the prophet and God wage that also rages within us all.

The book of Jonah throws the reader immediately into the prophet's call and his resistance. The word of God comes to Jonah, who is told to rise and go to an ancient city first mentioned early in Genesis (10:12). The story does away with the usual genealogical background because we have met Jonah earlier, in II Kings. There Jonah is mentioned as a prophet under King Jeroboam II of Samaria, a ruler who, we are told explicitly, did not depart from the sins of his ancestors. In the eighth century before the Common Era, Jonah's singular contribution to the reign of Jeroboam was to help the king recover territory lost to Israel: "It was he who restored the territory of Israel from Lebo-hamath to the sea of the Araba, in accordance with the promise that the Lord made through His servant, the prophet Jonah, son of Amitai, from Gath-hepher. For the Lord saw the plight of Israel, with neither bond nor free left and none to help Israel" (II Kings 14:25). God here is depicted as a compassionate ruler who helped Israel when its people lacked all other advocates. The prophet worked within the political confines of his day as an agent of God's mission.

Gath-hepher, Jonah's hometown, is near the city of Nazareth today, which explains why Jonah had to go down to Jaffa onto a ship: Jaffa was located to the south of his hometown. This passage may also help us understand Jonah's hesitation. Thus far, Jonah had been involved solely with strengthening and recovering the boundaries of Israel at a time of Israelite vulnerability. To task him with going to an enemy nation – one that had turned on the Jews time and again – in order to strengthen them morally could only undermine responsibilities he fulfilled in his past. Jonah was figuratively at sea and would soon be literally there as well.

Jonah's descent into Jaffa and then into the boat presages the deeper descent that he experienced; he also went down into the recesses of the ship and then down into a deep sleep. The Hebrew root y-r-d ("descend" or "go down") is repeated as the prophet sinks lower and lower into what today might be categorized as depression. He lacked even the most basic instinct of self-preservation, as he fell into what is nearly a comatose state while the ship was at breaking point. The captain was so intrigued by Jonah's behavior that he left his urgent responsibilities to wake the sleeping prophet with the question that rings in the ears of every penitent this season: "How can you be sleeping so soundly?" (Jonah 1:6). Many commentators see the ship's captain as the ultimate metaphor for God Himself. The captain gave Jonah the same command as God did earlier: Get up!

But Jonah was not able to rise to the occasion or help the sailors save themselves and the ship. His compassion for them was masked by his self-absorption. He had no room for pity, only self-pity. Instead, Jonah gave them enigmatic answers to very clear questions. Earlier, when asked what he did, he could not offer a straight answer. He said, "I am a Hebrew. I worship the Lord, the God of heaven, who made both sea and dry land" (1:9). This is hardly a job description. The only directive he was able to muster was the command that they throw him overboard. This is the ultimate statement of passivity, not even taking responsibility for one's own death. At a time when the sailors were focused on salvation, he asked them to be murderers, rather than just jumping overboard himself. They pressed their oars harder into the sea but to no avail. The tempest heightened in scale and intensity, and with a plea that God forgive them for any transgression of innocent blood spilled, they threw this odd man into the sea. When the sea ceased raging, the sailors offered sacrifices to Jonah's God, fearing Him in a way that Jonah did not. The chapter ends with their vows to God, an odd bookend to Jonah, who never paid his pledge and was now edging towards the bottom of the sea.

The contrast could not be greater. The sailors became a niggling foil for Jonah's recidivism. Later, the citizens of Nineveh would serve the same purpose, prompting ancient Christian scholars to take the critical view of this ancient prophet, arguing that it shows the fault lines of Jewish leadership.

The complexity of Jonah's inner battle is exquisitely captured in an engraving by French artist Gustav Doré (1832–1883). In the engraving, Jonah looks back in horror as he grips a scrim of dry land, the shore's edge of Nineveh, while the great leviathan of the sea turns to make its way back to the heart of the ocean.

Jonah Cast Forth by the Whale, Gustave Doré

It has just deposited Jonah on dry land. In Doré's engraving, the prophet's feet are only inches from the water and make a straight and invisible line to the great fish's tail, as if man and beast are aligned in mission. But Jonah finds himself alone in this artistic composition, clinging to the shore with a muscular arm; the folds of his tunic and the curls in his hair blend into the seamless flow of undulating dry land and cresting sea waters. The prophet looks as if he might lose his hold and slip into the sea's inky blackness. Jonah was no stranger to the waves, willing as he was to submit to them to quell the ocean squall that bubbled over when he ran away from God. Jonah, slipping back into the sea that saved him, is an apt metaphor for a man running far from his destiny, looking backwards without advancing, doubting his competence. He is painfully lonely.

But God's message was unambiguous: You cannot run. You cannot hide. Wherever you go, I will find you. I will use all of the natural world to force you to confront your self-doubts or your doubts about the sincerity of others: the big fish, the small worm, the East wind, the fast-growing tree, the burning sun. All of these were in God's arsenal to stop the prophet from his great escape. Jonah needed to go to Nineveh to deliver a message of destruction that would evolve into a charge of deliverance. God was willing to invest every resource to ensure that Jonah engaged his task. He used them all. God's insistence was not a form of punishment. It was an ongoing gift of compassion for the prophet to help model, nurture, and grow an impulse of grace that Jonah sorely lacked.

Doré shows us the moment of immense fright that leaves Jonah submerged with every one of his fears. The fish's fins are up as it rides off into the horizon. Water curls in two looping fountains from the fish's submerged head. The great fish has dropped Jonah off at the original destination, a mission Jonah tried to sail away from by boat. Deposited on the shores of Nineveh, Jonah glances back at this unique transportation service with what almost looks like longing. Jonah's eyes may either reflect the terror of what he has been through in this mammal's insides or the worry of leaving the protection of the great beast for the complicated task ahead. The artist leaves us to decide what troubles the prophet confronts on this foreign soil. Perhaps Doré took his cue from chapter two, Jonah's prayer inside the great fish.

Chapter two of Jonah has been regarded by many Bible scholars as a literary interpolation of a psalm-like passage, oddly interrupting the narrative arc of the story. And yet, Jonah's prayer itself offers great insight into the interior of a person running away from his mission. Jonah takes us on a virtual tour of the drowning process, frightening as it was. He first relays how the flood water swallowed him on the crest of the waves as he was heaved over. He then describes how "breakers and billows swept over" him. At that moment, at the initial descent, he presents his mental state: "I thought I was driven away, out of Your sight. Would I ever gaze again upon Your holy Temple?" (2:5). He understood for the first time the consequences of dying when the reality of the water's perils finally engulfed him. This was it. Life was nearly over. All of the consequences of non-existence faced him squarely. He descended further: "The waters closed in over me. The deep engulfed me. Weeds twined around my head. I sank to the base of the mountains; the bars of the earth closed upon me forever" (2:6–7). Finally, there was nowhere he could run. Seaweed twisted about him as he sank lower and lower. He had literally sunk to the base of the earth. The waters closed in on him and then the sand bars at the sea's very bottom. There was no lower place for him to go.

Many of us fail to realize Jonah's point of salvation because we never ask when the fish swallowed Jonah. But the prayer tells us. He was at the lowest possible point before being saved. Like so many who run far away from their life's purpose, he needed to sink to the very bottom before the text could record his praise of God: "Yet You brought my life up from the pit, O Lord my God! When my life was ebbing away, I called to the Lord" (2:7–8). Life was ebbing away. He was saved suddenly and unexpectedly but only when he had nowhere else to go. That is when God showed him ultimate compassion and sent an agent of salvation.

Jonah translated the compassion he received into a commitment to fulfill his mission. The fish transported him to Nineveh, and he surfaced on dry land ostensibly a new man, dedicated to God's word. Doré's only other depiction of Jonah is in Nineveh itself. The prophet's arms are outstretched, and the look of woe on his face communicates to those seated all around him that life is soon to be dramatically altered. His pronouncement is not long and flowing, as in the words of prophets like Ezekiel or Isaiah. It is short and to the point: "Forty days more and Nineveh shall be overturned" (3:4). In *Four Strange Books of the Bible,* Elias Bickerman notes this change of prophetic message.[1] The new, direct, and abbreviated style causes the prophet even further worry. Unlike the parables and similes of other prophets, Jonah's directive contains no blurring or fogginess. Nothing is left open to interpretation. Jonah articulated a message that is cutting and sure: "Forty days more and Nineveh shall be overturned."

Contrast Jonah's surety to two strange appearances of doubt that appear in two of the book's four chapters. When the boat carrying Jonah is about to capsize because of the tempest at sea, the captain tells Jonah to pray because perhaps they will all be saved as a result. Later, the king of Nineveh commands his entire city and its animals to fast and improve their ways: "Who knows but that God may turn and relent?" (3:9). Both authority figures bank on God's compassion, a compassion that God eventually extends. In contrast, Jonah, trapped in the black-and-white mindset of justice alone, is sure that there is no chance of salvation. The compassion God extends to Jonah has no long-lasting impact on the prophet's capacity for compassion.

When Jonah barks out his prophecy, he has only one meaning in mind. "Forty days more and Nineveh shall be overturned" can only mean, in his mind, that the city will be destroyed. But the clever semantic understanding of "overturned" in Hebrew implies reversal as well. In forty days, destruction can become salvation if everyone repents. In Doré's Nineveh, some of the town's citizens look at the prophet with visible tension. Others cup their heads in their hands in despair. Some look bored, as if Hebrew prophets regularly visited the area with apocalyptic messages; one listener in Doré's engraving stands at the prophet's feet with one hand on his hip as if to say to the prophet, "I do not believe you."

And there is another troubling detail, so small we might easily overlook it as yet another subtle statement of Jonah's hesitation. Nineveh, we learn in chapter three, was "enormously large, a three days' walk across" (3:3). Details like this rarely appear in the Bible and make us question their necessity – until we are told that Jonah made only one day's walk into the city when he proclaimed the prophecy that swept like wildfire through this vast, ancient city. Jonah walked no further into Nineveh. He stepped out of it quickly, doubting the authenticity of the city's repentance. Arguably, Jonah did not need to journey deeper into the heart of Nineveh because his word traveled quickly, penetrating the immoral surfaces of person and animal alike. But perhaps he could not go any further. He tried to muster the courage and resilience to abide by a mission he never asked for and initially rejected. But he could not carry it through. His hesitation appears in his footsteps – or lack of them. He had no love for these foreigners, no desire to see them transform themselves. He wanted to leave the city with haste before God did to Nineveh what he once did to Sodom and Gomorrah. In Jonah's mind, justice would prevail.

Jonah's name is mentioned in the book whose title bears his

name; he is also referred to in II Kings as the son of Amitai, a figure we do not encounter in the Bible. The notion of being the "Son of Truth," playing off the root e-m-t ("truth") of Amitai's name, offers the reader a paradox. Jonah, a child of truth, ran away from his God-given destiny. As such, his end could come to no good. Later, in the fourth chapter, as he offered a puzzling explanation for his escape, he reviewed God's qualities as listed in Exodus 34:6, namely that God is compassionate and long-suffering. But whereas in Exodus the list ends with God as faithful or truthful, Jonah omitted the word "*emet*" in his description. Jonah was angry; he believed that God was much more compassionate than honest. An honest God would have held the Ninevites accountable not only for their many sins but for a repentance that seemed shallow and incomplete. In the Exodus verse, this inequality of descriptors bears out. God is described as truthful only once but as merciful multiple times.

We review this set of verses again and again during the *seliḥot* period and in our recitations on *Ne'ila*:

> The Lord! The Lord! A God compassionate and gracious, slow to anger, abounding in kindness and truth, extending kindness to the thousandth generation, forgiving iniquity, transgression and sin, yet He does not remit all punishment. (Exodus 34:6–7)

On Yom Kippur, we ask that God display this mercy in abundant ways, pushing aside our wrongs and extending grace to us, even though we do not deserve it. Herein lay Jonah's greatest flaw as leader. He wanted justice for others and compassion for himself. He almost called God a liar for being too merciful when God should have judged harshly. Jonah judged God, believing that God's compassion was a weak impulse when justice should have been served instead. Jonah could not face the truth of his own leadership failure and projected it onto God.

But when it came to truth-telling, God showed Jonah that true leadership lies in balancing justice with compassion. Jonah moved east of Nineveh and made a *sukka* for himself, a small booth that symbolized his removal and enclosure from the place he left; from this observation point, he watched what would happen to the city, convinced that if God gave the city forty days until it was destroyed He would indeed destroy it. But then God gave Jonah a *kikayon*, a tree described in the Talmud as offering shade and medicinal properties. It was not as sparse as his *sukka*. Jonah was happy for the first time in his recorded history. The only happiness Jonah expresses in the entire book was over this tree.

When God removed the tree that Jonah had not planted or nurtured, Jonah was so despondent that he questioned his very life:

> He begged for death, saying, "I would rather die than live." Then God said to Jonah, "Are you so deeply grieved about the plant?" "Yes," he replied, "so deeply that I want to die." (4:8–9)

Jonah's request is shocking. How can it be that Jonah felt so aggrieved over a plant that he did not enjoy for more than a day? Jonah's plant spared him discomfort, the text tells us, but it symbolized much more. It was a sign of God's grace and love. When it was removed, Jonah felt the blazing sun beating on his head and felt faint.

> Then the Lord said, "You cared about the plant, which you did not work for and which you did not grow, which appeared overnight and perished overnight. And should I not care about Nineveh, that great city, in which there are more than a hundred and twenty thousand persons who do not yet know their right hand from their left and many beasts as well?" (4:10–11)

Jonah wanted the protection of a tree he did not deserve. The tree made him happy. He wanted the gift of something he did not deserve.

A prophet who runs away from the Lord should not get presents; he should get punished. God understood Jonah's anguish and sought to relieve it by teaching Jonah the most basic lesson of compassion. Jonah wanted pity, mercy, nurturing, and protection – all aspects of love and caring that we receive from others – which he did not merit. Yet he could not extend that gift of mercy to others. And in that failure, he betrayed his job as a prophet. A prophet can give a sincere message only when he feels the intensity of its repercussions and wants only the best for those he berates. The ideal prophet and leader wants to praise people more than he wants to criticize them. Jonah wanted love but could not give it. We, the readers, have no idea if Jonah was ever able to muster that mercy because God gets the last word in the book.

Jonah is everyman. We, too, want the gift of grace, a present we do not deserve, a reprieve from a crime that merits punishment. We want the police officer to forget about the speeding ticket and just issue a warning even though we know we drove over the limit. The officer is justified in giving us that ticket. It is only our good luck on occasion when he smiles instead and tells us to be careful next time.

Jonah continues to confound. Yet a flawed prophet's tale of rejection, hesitation, and acceptance found an important place in the biblical canon and plays a central role on Yom Kippur afternoon. We, the penitents in Jonah's shadow, know all too well the challenge of change. We, too, reject our calling and question it, resist destiny, hesitate, drag our feet, capitulate, and stand back in anguish looking at the sum total of our accomplishments. We question God's ways, sometimes evading the questions we must really ask ourselves. We all have moments when we judge the loyalty of a friend, the commitment of a spouse, the responsibility of a child, the purpose of our existence. When we enter these dark spaces, we rarely see the sin of it. We experience self-pity. In the space where self-pity lives, teshuva cannot live. There is no room for change when we feel sorry for ourselves. And like the book of Jonah, we close Yom Kippur with God's question: Can we really hope for change when we want compassion for ourselves but demand justice for others?

LIFE HOMEWORK

We are all running away from something. Is there something you are running away from facing right now? Why? What would it take to do an about-face and confront the problem? Think about having the strength this season to do that.

Now think of a situation this past year when you needed more compassion. What did it feel like to be denied the nurturing that compassion brings with it? Consider someone who needs compassion from you right now. Why are you withholding it? Transfer your need for compassion to the person you are denying compassion to who needs it from you. Hold back on judgment for the moment and try to imitate the grace we associate with God in our prayers during these Days of Awe. Imitating God, our mandate from the first chapter of Genesis, means having a deep well of compassion.

PASSAGES FOR ADDITIONAL STUDY

Maimonides, *Mishneh Torah, The Laws of Repentance* 5:4

> Were God to decree that an individual would be righteous or wicked or that there would be a quality which draws a person by his essential nature to any particular path [of behavior], set of ideals, attributes, or deeds, as imagined by many of the fools [who believe] in astrology – how could He command us through [the words of] the prophets: "Do this," "Do not do this," "Improve your behavior," or "Do not follow after your wickedness?".... What place would there be for the entire Torah? According to which judgment or sense of justice would retribution be administered to the wicked or reward to the righteous? Shall the whole world's Judge not act justly!

Rabbi Moshe Haim Luzzatto, *The Path of the Just*,
Chapter 25: "The Manner of Acquiring Fear of Sin"

> Once it has become clear to one that wherever he may be, he is standing before the Presence of the Blessed One, there will come to him of itself, the fear and trepidation of going astray in

his actions so that they do not accord with the majesty of the Blessed One. As it is stated (*Ethics of the Fathers* 2:1), "Know what is above you: a seeing eye, a listening ear, and a book in which all your deeds are inscribed." And they are all inscribed in a book, whether they be in one's favor or against him.

Rabbi Abraham Isaac Kook, *The Lights of Repentance* 7:5

At the time that a man sins he is in "the world of separation," and then every detail stands by itself, and evil is evil by itself and it possesses evil and harmful value. When he repents out of love, there immediately shines upon him the essential light of the "world of unity," where all is interwoven into one form. In the general relationship there is no evil at all, for evil combines with virtue to facilitate and exalt even further the significant worth of goodness. Thereby are intentionally evil deeds transformed into veritable deeds of merit.

Text questions to think about while studying:

- We have to have the freedom to run away if we believe in free will. We also have to understand the consequences of free will. How do the sources above contribute to our understanding of free will?
- How does "knowing what is above you" force compassion?
- What does it mean to repent out of love?

Notes

1. Elias Bickerman, *Four Strange Books of the Bible* (New York: Schocken Books, 1985).

Day Six

Gratitude

"For the sin we committed before You by insufficient respect for parents and teachers."

The first words out of the mouth of a traditional Jew upon waking are: "I am grateful," *Modeh Ani*. It is not merely a prayer. It is a personal statement of being. It is a reflection on abundance before we have even engaged the world. We are grateful merely for the *fact* of our existence. "I give thanks to You, living and everlasting King, for You have restored my soul with mercy. Great is Your faithfulness." My soul has been restored. I can live another day.

Yet as we travel through the rest of the day and face the prosaic cares it spews forth, we understand that rather than set the tone for the day, *Modeh Ani* can feel like a momentary aberration. A day full of gratitude seems increasingly unlikely. We said thank you once and first but may hear and say it less as the hours pass.

Most people fail to get the recognition they deserve for the work they do or for the small kindnesses they attempt. We even find ourselves saying, "no good deed goes unpunished" a little too often. Not only will goodness not be acknowledged, it may bring some trouble in its wake. The first time I heard this expression as an adult, I thought it was a mistake. Surely, good deeds go unpunished. They get rewarded. The person must have gotten it wrong. But then as some of the veneer of innocence peeled off, I came to understand that this is often a thankless world and that we must nurture ourselves because we may not get the support we need from others. Good things we do go misunderstood or undervalued. This erosion of faith in others can turn optimists into pessimists and pessimists into nihilists.

The bankruptcy of gratitude is always an enigma. Philosopher David Hume in *A Treatise of Human Nature* believed that ingratitude was the ugliest of human behaviors: "Of all crimes that human creatures are capable of committing, the most horrid and unnatural is ingratitude, especially when it is committed against parents, and appears in the more flagrant instances of wounds and death."[1] The incapacity to thank others was deemed unnatural by Hume, implying that the impulse to be grateful stems from some genuinely loving instinct that is somehow obstructed. Ingratitude towards parents was particularly problematic for Hume. Although parents get no formal training for the job and many fall short of its incredible emotional and physical demands, for Hume, at least parents bring you into the world. The appreciation we owe parents – in some ways the human equivalent to the *Modeh Ani,* which demands gratitude before we even start the day – is first and foremost for the fact that we could not exist without them, notwithstanding all the sacrifices that they make or made to ensure that we have life's necessities and its many bonuses.

Hume's implication would seem counter to what we hear many times a day. We hear people say thank you all the time. We thank people, but thanking them is not necessarily recognizing them. Hume was scratching beneath the surface of petty formalities. We often thank people because it is expected. It is part of being polite. It is on the agenda for a meeting, scripted and prepared. Sometimes the thank you is prewritten, ready to offer when the evening is over, the event is done, the exchange is completed. A full sentence was cropped to two words, then one word, and then finally one word with no vowels: thnx. Too much is missing, and it's more than a vowel that we lack. These empty words are not spontaneous, extemporaneous, or fresh. Some thank yous feel stale and insincere.

Worse is that many thank yous are really hidden requests for something else, like acknowledgment letters from charities that are really just another solicitation. Veteran fundraiser Jerold Panas believes that donors must be thanked seven times to feel appropriately recognized.[2] Maybe people need to be thanked multiple times because they really feel they haven't been thanked at all.

What explains this lack of appreciation or our incapacity to express gratitude sincerely, specifically, and robustly, especially if it is deemed unnatural to lack gratitude? Robert Solomon in *The Psychology of Gratitude* ponders this very matter in his foreword to the book:

> The neglect of gratitude is, in itself, interesting.... We do not like to think of ourselves as indebted. We would rather see our good fortunes as our own doing.... Like the emotion of trust, it invokes an admission of our vulnerability and our dependence on other people. Thus gratitude lies at the very heart of ethics. It is more basic, perhaps, than even duty and obligation.[3]

We may not consciously think of gratitude as an act of vulnerability, but it is a statement of need and dependence that some may rather dismiss than admit. We hear variations of this all of the time:

"That's what any child should do for his parents."

"I don't have to thank her. She gets a paycheck."

"He knows he did a good job. He doesn't need me to tell him."

"I don't want her head to get so big it can't get through the door."

Really?

This emotional stinginess is not helped by the fact that those who may have received little praise as children have decided unconsciously to pay the debt forward. "I didn't get a thank you. Why should you?" This deficit-based way of interacting is highly flawed; it serves only to diminish others and, in so doing, diminishes our own sense of abundance and blessing.

Psychoanalyst Melanie Klein, in *Envy and Gratitude,* writes that gratitude may be an admission that you are better than me. Envy, she writes, stems from a sense that love or material gain that should be given to me has been stolen by you. I cannot stand the sight of your enjoyment, only your misery, because your happiness should rightfully have been mine. Klein believes that envy is a response to profound childhood needs that went unfulfilled and are insatiable because the person who envies others "can never be satisfied because his envy comes from within and, therefore, always finds an object to focus on."[4] If I thank you for your advice, wisdom, energy, or friendship, I may be admitting that you have something I do not have. Because I may be mindful of your talents and abilities in relation to my own, my thank you may be a way that I confess to my own insecurities or inadequacies. I may not have enough self-confidence to acknowledge your importance in my life. "Gratitude is closely bound up with generosity," Klein writes, stating that those who possess inner wealth can share their gifts easily with others and feel enriched as a result.[5] Those who lack this inner wealth may give to others but then have an exaggerated need for appreciation because of an anxiety that they have been "impoverished and robbed." Depletion must be immediately filled.

Managing jealousy, greed, and envy – linked emotions for Klein – is difficult; all serve as obstacles to an attitude of gratitude. But because gratitude is so seminal to the religious life, we have to overcome our own limitations and learn how to extend it with authenticity and force. The Christian mystic Meister Eckhart (1260–1327) once wrote: "If the only prayer you said in your whole life was, 'thank you,' that would suffice." Thank you *does* mean that I need you or that I am vulnerable or that I cannot function without help. It means that we live in the presence of others and that life in community is inherently about dependence. Thank you is an expression of relationship. It reveals the dependence we have on each other, even if a certain toughness of spirit prevents us, at times, from acknowledging it.

This sense of dependence is rendered powerfully in a prayer recited multiple times a day in traditional circles: the *Modim*, a statement of thanks that appears in the *Amida* (eighteen benedictions). Repeating it creates a pause at daily intervals to bow the knee low with humility and indebtedness:

> We are thankful to You that You, Adonai, are our God and the God of our fathers, forever – Rock of our lives, Shield of our deliverance, You are in every generation. We will give thanks to You and recount Your praise, for our lives which are committed into Your hand, and for our souls which are entrusted to You, and for Your miracles of every day with us, and for Your wonders and benefactions at all times – evening, morning, and noon. You the Beneficent One – for Your compassion is never withheld. You are the Merciful One – for Your kindness never ceases; we have always placed our hope in You.

Evening, morning, and noon the miracles keep coming, and the lives and souls that we entrust to God are renewed, as is our hope. Notice how many times the word "You" appears in the prayer, while any reference to the self never makes an appearance.

This liturgical recitation of thanks has its High Holiday parallel. The *piyut*, or acrostic poem, "*Imru L'Elohim*," affirms the obligation to praise God for an act of creation and sustenance, coupling it in each stanza with gratitude that God is forgiving and pardons our sins. We thank God for making us and then for our capacity to remake ourselves in God's image:

> Praise God!
> He made all things with His word,
> And He performed and accomplished [all],
> He pardons the nation that He carries;
> Therefore, His people trust in Him.
> Remember the wonders He has performed.

We are asked to remember God's wonders because this memory will generate more appreciation than we already feel.

Thanking God should spill over to the way that we thank human beings, but even those who pray these words with piety can scrimp when it comes to gratitude to a friend. Bahya ibn Pakuda, an eleventh-century Spanish scholar who wrote what many consider to be the first systematic work of Jewish philosophy, *Duties of the Heart*, offers a cogent explanation of this disparity. *Duties of the Heart* has become a staple of *Musar* literature and the yeshiva curriculum and has remained one of the chief works of ethical influence for centuries. Ibn Pakuda wrote it, he states in his introduction, because people were becoming overly concerned with the duties of the body (*ḥovot ha'evarim*) and its many demands while ignoring the duties of the heart (*ḥovot halevavot*). For ibn Pakuda, known affectionately as Bahya in most scholarly circles, thanksgiving was considered an important duty of the heart, and no Jewish heart is complete without an understanding of how interrelated belief is with gratitude. Bahya also understood that there are many utilitarian motives behind the kindnesses we extend to each other and the thanks that subsequently result:

> When we consider the favors men do for each other, we find them all falling under one of five following categories: first, the favors done by parent for child; second, those done by a master for a slave; third, favors done by the wealthy for the poor, for the sake of heavenly rewards; fourth, favors done by one person for another for the sake of praise, honor, and earthly rewards; and fifth, those done by the powerful for the sake of the weak, out of pity and compassion.[6]

In each of these relationships, there is an imbalance of power that precipitates giving. A parent gives to a child out of responsibility; a master gives to his slave out of self-interest. The noble take care of the poor out of hope to get in God's divine graces; people are kind to one another for praise or status. Sometimes kindness emerges out of compassion. If each of these human relationships generates appreciation, Bahya observed, then all of these impulses are even truer in relation to God:

> How much more then, should a person obey, praise, and thank the Creator for all benefaction and benefactors, whose beneficence is infinite, permanent and perpetual, done neither for His own benefit nor for driving away misfortunes, but His all-loving kindness and grace towards people.[7]

The thank you that we give others is no match for the thank you that we owe God, who has no precipitating reason to bestow kindness upon us. It is all out of grace. If we can muster the thoughtfulness to understand this, the spillover impact is immense. If we can wrap ourselves around the fact that no one owes us kindness – it is all beyond what we deserve – then any kindness becomes an object worthy of acknowledgement. The physician and theologian Albert Schweitzer (1875–1965) confirms Bahya's sentiment: "Nothing that is done for you is a matter of course. Everything originates in a will for the good, which is directed at you. Train yourself never to put off the word or action for the expression of gratitude."

Bahya's understanding limns our reading of Judaism's most famous expression of gratitude: *Dayenu*, the musical centerpiece of the Haggada. Virtually every commentator on this passage observes that we would *not* have thought it enough had God freed us from slavery but not given us a Torah. We would not be who we are without each stage in our historical progression, but *Dayenu* forces us to pause and underline those stages, understanding their causal relationship for the whole of our identity and appreciating that had God stopped at any stage, we would never have actualized the much larger vision of our spiritual and national agenda. While we never utter the Hebrew word for thanks in the song, we do not need to because we are *makir tov*, we recognize the good of the Exodus by acknowledging God's hand in our salvation again and again:

> How many kindnesses has God shown us!
> If He had brought us out of Egypt but did not judge the Egyptians, it would have been enough.
> If He had judged the Egyptians but not judged their gods, it would have been enough....
> If He had given us the Torah but had not brought us to the land of Israel, it would have been enough.
> If He had brought us to the land of Israel but did not build the Temple for us, it would have been enough....
> How much more so do we owe thanks to God for His repeated and manifold favors to us! That He brought us out of Egypt... and he gave us the Torah, and...

Solomon Schimmel, in his article "Gratitude in Judaism," comments on the unique structure of *Dayenu* as a model for expressing gratitude: "When we reflect on a benefit that God [or by extension, another person] has done for us, we should break it into its multiple components, meditating on each element."[8]

Can we say a better thank you? *Dayenu* tells us we can and that we must. When we sing the praises of others generously and specifically, we do more than offer them a gift. We open up our own world of plenitude, revealing to ourselves the great fortune that is ours, even amidst hardship. As contemporary writer Melodie Beattie observes: "Gratitude unlocks the fullness of life. It turns what we have into enough, and more." *Dayenu.*

A thank you is most impactful when it identifies aspects of the recipient's help or participation that are not obvious. Appreciation affects us most when we expect it least. In classes on the subject, I often ask students to write a thank you note to someone who is not expecting it, and offer time in class to write and read the notes, if participants want to share. One woman wrote a thank you note for someone who helped her cope with a difficult illness; she began to cry as she read what she wrote. Through tears, she said it made her feel good to write it. The note was not only for the recipient. It was also for the giver. She needed to feel the bounty of life, not despite her health struggle, but because of it. She needed to see beyond tragedy to a world of affirming kindnesses. *Dayenu.*

Dayenu teaches us that we need to be grateful immediately after an act of kindness and also to be thankful in the long-term for how all of those acts come together to form who we are. At every interval in life's journey, a thank you forces a pause of meaning, an interruption that stops us on the path and makes us stand still. And this helps us better understand why we confess every Yom Kippur for not respecting our parents and teachers sufficiently. More than anyone else, they guide us through often painful and difficult passages of time when we need to grow emotionally and intellectually. We may blame them or harbor anger at one stage of our growth, then later come to appreciate the very prodding that at an earlier stage bewildered or troubled us. They are with us for the long haul. *Dayenu.*

Ruth Fainlight is a contemporary English poet, writer, and translator. She, too, helps us stop and savor the moment. She helps us look up in this season of judgment and offer praise:

> Nothing ever happens more than once.
> The next time is never like before.
> What you thought you learned doesn't apply.
> Something is different. And just as real.
> For which you might be thankful after all.

LIFE HOMEWORK

As we confess any disrespect we show to parents or teachers, two figures of authority in our lives, let's redeem any hurt by acknowledging the goodness of parents and teachers in making us who we are. We often take these relationships for granted; we may disrespect them simply through a failure to acknowledge them. Even if relationships are strained or difficult, we can always find qualities to admire. Sometimes growing that admiration becomes the opening for a new kind of relationship.

Take out three pieces of your nicest stationery and three stamps.

First Note: Write a thank you note to your parents (or one of your parents). You couldn't possibly capture all that they have done for you but try the *dayenu* technique. Think of several ways that your parents have influenced you and include them all. The more specific you are, the more your thank you will have impact and meaning. Make this the note that your parent will keep because it speaks of a bond that is unique. If your thank you note can be given to ten other people, it is not personal enough.

Second Note: Now write a note to a teacher who influenced you or modeled a special trait or taught you an important subject, even if it was a very long time ago. Try to track that teacher down. Tell this teacher what you are doing and how what they gave you helped make you into the person you are now. Great teachers are hard to find, but their names and positive associations stay with us for a lifetime. Teachers get so little thanks for growing us, but it's never too late to say thank you to them.

Third Note: In the spirit of surprise that makes a thank you meaningful, think of one person who deserves a thank you but who does not expect to hear from you right now.

PASSAGES FOR ADDITIONAL STUDY

Maimonides, *Mishneh Torah, The Laws of Repentance* 6:4

This is what is implied in the requests of the righteous and the prophets in their prayers, [asking] God to help them on the path of truth, as David pleaded [Psalms 86:11]: "God, show me Your way that I may walk in Your truth"; i.e., do not let my sins prevent me from [reaching] the path of truth which will lead me to appreciate Your way and the oneness of Your name. A similar intent [is conveyed] by the request [Psalms 51:14]: "Support me with a spirit of magnanimity"; i.e., let my spirit [be willing] to do Your will and do not cause my sins to prevent me from repenting. Rather, let the choice remain in my hand until I repent and comprehend and appreciate the path of truth…

Rabbi Moshe Haim Luzzatto, *The Path of the Just*, Chapter 10: "The Trait of Cleanliness"

Envy is nothing but want of reason and foolishness, for the one who envies gains nothing for himself and deprives the one he envies of nothing. He only loses, thereby, as is indicated in the verse that I mentioned (Job 5:2): "Envy kills the fool." There are those who are so foolish that if they perceive their neighbor to possess a certain good, they brood and worry and suffer to the point that their neighbor's good prevents them from enjoying their own.

Rabbi Abraham Isaac Kook, *The Lights of Repentance*, Chapter 3

There is a form of penitence that addresses itself to a particular sin or to many sins. The person confronts his sin face to face, and feels remorseful that he fell into the trap of sin. Slowly he struggles to come out of it, until he is liberated from his sinful enslavement and he begins to experience a holy freedom that is most delightful to his weary self. His healing continues; rays of a benign sun, bearing divine mercy, reach out to him, and a feeling of happiness grows within him…. His wistful spirit recalls with joyous relief its previous inner anguish, and is filled with a feeling of gratitude.

Text questions to think about while studying:

- How does walking in the way of God help you become more grateful?
- Why is envy the enemy of gratitude?
- What about teshuva makes you more grateful?

Notes

1. David Hume, *A Treatise of Human Nature* (New York: Oxford University Press USA, 2011), 300.
2. Jerold Panas, *The Fundraising Habits of Supremely Successful Boards* (Medfield, MA: Emerson and Church, 2006).
3. Robert Solomon, "Foreword," in *The Psychology of Gratitude*, ed. Robert A. Emmons and Michael E. McCullough (New York: Oxford University Press USA, 2004), v–vi.
4. Melanie Klein, *Envy and Gratitude* (London: Delacorte Press, 1963), 182. I am grateful to Joanne Cohen, who introduced me to this book.
5. Ibid., 189.
6. Bahya ibn Pakuda, *Duties of the Heart*, Treatise III, Introduction, as found in Louis Jacobs, *Jewish Ethics, Philosophy and Mysticism* (New York: Behrman House, 1969), 5–6.
7. Ibid., 8.
8. Solomon Schimmel, "Gratitude in Judaism," in *The Psychology of Gratitude*, ed. Robert A. Emmons and Michael E. McCullough (New York: Oxford University Press USA, 2004), 40.

Day Seven

Anger

"For the sin we committed before You with impudence."

Very soon, as we wind down the holiday season, we will complete our reading of the whole Torah and celebrate this accomplishment on Simḥat Torah. We close Deuteronomy 34, the very last chapter, with the death of Moses. It seems a fitting end: we close the book with the close of the life of its most central leader. Moses died fighting after struggling with a lifetime of anger management. Moses managed the anger of a people who complained incessantly about wilderness conditions. Moses managed God's anger after the golden calf incident and flare-ups throughout the trek, petitioning God to extend every reservoir of mercy to a wayward collection of ragtag travelers who had lost their way. And Moses had his own anger to manage – in the very same incident – when the tablets he brought down to edify, educate, and uplift the community suddenly seemed irrelevant, given the idolatrous leanings of the masses.

Moses' management of these competing angers was perhaps his most significant contribution to leadership; he was able to negotiate a peace broad enough to sustain fragile relationships over forty years. The anger was pervasive and profound, but it did not derail Moses' larger vision. It did, however, get in the way of Moses' personal crowning achievement: his own entrance into the land of Israel. When he hit the rock instead of speaking to it and called the people rebels, his anger merited a harsh punishment; he could see the land but not step into it. Anger always has a cost.

A small collection of midrashim called *Midrash Petirat Moshe* (midrashim on the death of Moses), probably written between the seventh and eleventh centuries, was first published in the sixteenth century in Constantinople, and it traced Moses' last hours. In this set of midrashim on Moses' demise, a *bat kol* ("heavenly voice") came down from the skies and said to Moses: "It is time for you to be taken from this world." Moses, it is time to go, the voice beckoned. Moses pleaded with God: "Remember the day when You revealed Yourself to me at the bush! Remember Sinai and the forty days and nights I spent there! Please, please don't turn me over to the Angel of Death."

When Moses realized that his supplication amounted to words in the wind, he used an unusual delaying tactic. He asked God if he could bless the Jewish people one more time, each tribe with a separate blessing. This would buy him more time. But just as he was in the midst of delivering his farewells, he saw that his time had almost run out. The Angel of Death was losing patience. Moses gathered everyone together quickly for one collective blessing. But, much as Jacob blessed his sons with many gloomy predictions about their future, Moses' blessing was no blessing. It was a request for *meḥila,* forgiveness: "I made you suffer to keep Torah and mitzvot," he said, *"ve'akhshav maḥlu li"* – now, grant me your forgiveness. And they said, *"Rabbenu ve'adonenu, maḥul lakh"* – we forgive you. Then the people cried out to Moses: "Moses, our teacher, we angered you and made your life difficult – forgive us." And he responded, "I forgive you." And then he was gone. Moses ran out of time. He used his very last breath to ask forgiveness from his people, and his people asked forgiveness from him. It was forgiveness for anger, an anger that trailed forty years of imposing – and questioning – authority.[1]

The relationship between anger and forgiveness is not hard to conjure. Anger that feels uncontrollable often gets resolved in a passionate and meaningful display of contrition. The vehemence of anger often turns into the desperate plea to be forgiven, substituting one intensity of emotion for another. But the pattern of sin, anger, exile, and forgiveness is so well established in life and in biblical history that it wearies us and makes us wonder if it will ever come to an end. Are we destined to replay it constantly, much like someone in an abusive relationship characterized by violence followed by forgiveness? The pattern emotionally exhausts and depletes its victims and often its perpetrators.

This midrash may sound like the happy ending we wanted for our venerable leader, but in reality, there is something exceptionally tragic about it. A forty-year tumultuous relationship ended with an apology with only minutes left to a life. Had Moses both asked for forgiveness and granted it earlier, he could have put the anger behind him and enjoyed a changed relationship. He may even have been buried in the Promised Land.

In *The Path of the Just*, Rabbi Moshe Haim Luzzatto delineates different types of anger, loosely based on the following saying from *Ethics of the Fathers*:

> There are four types of temperaments. One who is easily angered and easily appeased – his virtue cancels his flaw. One whom it is difficult to anger and difficult to appease – his flaw cancels his virtue. One whom it is difficult to anger and is easily appeased is pious. One who is easily angered and is difficult to appease is wicked. (5:14)

All anger is not the same.

Rabbi Luzzatto then creates anger profiles to help this passage become more clear and descriptive. The category names are mine; the quotations are from *The Path of the Just*.

FURY

The first type of anger is fury. Any opposition to the will of a furious person is met with intimidating wrath, to the degree that "his heart is no longer with him and his judgment vanishes."[2] Anger clouds rationality and is a force so potent in the person of fury that he is almost unrecognizable; his state of anger is entirely different from his normal temperament. It is this kind of anger that our sages probably thought of when one remarked: "A person who is angry it is as if he worshipped idols."[3] The anger described here is so intense and destructive that Rabbi Luzzatto feared the worst for those caught in the cyclone of its path: "A man such as he would destroy the entire world if it were within his power to do so, for he is not in any way directed by reason and is as devoid of sensibility as any predatory beast."[4] This kind of anger is primal and animalistic. It surges forth indiscriminately, and Rabbi Luzzatto worried that in the state of rage, a person with this kind of anger could commit any number of heinous crimes.

Because fury has such a transformative impact on its victims, those who suffer this type of anger will often apologize profusely: "I don't know what happened to me" or "I didn't mean it." And in some odd way, they may be right. The rabid, apoplectic person that spewed out venom is not the same person when contrite. Anger has so wholly taken over that the individual becomes unrecognizable. But when this happens more than once without sufficient accountability, the apologies stop working. No one believes the perpetrator.

SLOW BURN

This anger is not easily ignited but burns hot once it is. In the words of *Ethics of the Fathers*, this state belongs to one who is slow to anger. Unlike the person of fury whose anger is easily set off and takes a long time to wear off, the worst of possible conditions, this individual does not need to control every small point or react to everything that might get under his skin. Slow burn takes time to gather its forces, but when it does it is relentless and destructive. The anger is just as virulent when it hits as it is in the first case. It is so damaging that "he will not afterwards be able to straighten what he has made crooked."[5] We can do damage control for slights and mild insults, but fits of anger like these stay imprinted on the memory of others like a Rorschach blot of bitterness, as it says in Job, "Envy kills the fool" (Job 5:2). Many relationships are killed by anger.

RESTRAINED ANGER

Anger that is not easily aroused, and even when aroused is restrained, represents for Rabbi Luzzatto a higher level of self-control. This type of anger does not descend into irrationality, yet the one who has it is still called "a man of anger"[6] because he nurses his wrath. Rather than a slow burn, it is more like a simmer. The person has less to lose than his angrier friends, but he is still touched and moved by his anger in some way. Rabbi Luzzatto places this entire discussion in his chapter on cleanliness. Here he refers not to physical hygiene but to certain negative character traits and what we look like when we have managed to clean ourselves of even the slightest smack of their deleterious effects. A person clean of anger has no simmering anger. It comes and goes. It does not linger.

APPROPRIATE ANGER

It is hard to think of any expression of anger as appropriate, but Rabbi Luzzatto did not recommend placidity and passivity in the face of outrage or in instances when passion can become an important educational tool, as in a teaching or parenting relationship. Controlled anger may be necessary to ensure that an important life message penetrates the heart and mind of the listener. In this instance, *The Path of the Just* recommends, "Any anger shown... should be anger of the face and not anger of the heart."[7] This individual may experience anger, but it is not consuming. It takes a long time for anger to surface, and it is quickly let go into the ether where it flies away before doing any real damage. A person who can achieve this level of control and relinquishment is worthy of Rabbi Luzzatto's praise. This is reminiscent of a statement made by the sage Adda ben Ahaba: "Anger never went to bed with me."[8] He did not say that he never experienced anger, only that it was not his company in the middle of the night. Adda ben Ahaba was not lying in his bed stewing with glowering insomnia. Contrast this to a refrigerator magnet: "Don't go to sleep angry. Stay up and fight."

Rabbi Luzzatto concludes this section of his writing with a famous talmudic quote about the signature of a person as he or she walks in the world: "A person is recognized in three ways: through his goblet, through his pocket, and through his anger."[9] A goblet can refer to the way a person holds his drink according to some commentaries.

To others, it refers to the way we share the food at our table: if our cup truly runneth over, then we openly share our abundance with others. The pocket refers to our philanthropic giving. We are judged not by what we have but ultimately by what we give away. And the last hallmark of our footprint in this world is the way we manage our anger. It's as simple and as difficult as that.

Hundreds of years before Rabbi Luzzatto offered his commentary on this passage from *Ethics of the Fathers,* Nahmanides wrote an ethical will to his son, "In Praise of Humility." His chief concern was that his son understand the relationship between anger and humility and remind himself continually about the importance of self-control. Nahmanides even advised his son to read the letter weekly to keep its content fresh in his mind as a guardian over his behavior. The letter became so popular that it is included in many prayerbooks. These excerpts illustrate Nahmanides' understanding of anger as a manifestation of the ego:

> "Hear, my son, the instruction of your father, and forsake not the teaching of your mother" (Proverbs 1:8). Train yourself always to speak softly to every man. You will then avoid anger for which there is no worse trait for it brings a man to sin. Our Rabbis said: "Whoever flies into a rage, every kind of Hell has dominion over him." As it is said: "Therefore remove anger from your heart, and put away evil from your flesh" (Ecclesiastes 11:10)....
>
> And when you are saved from anger your heart will embrace the trait of humility, which is the finest of all good traits, as it is said: "The reward of humility is the fear of the Lord" (Proverbs 22:4). As a result of humility the fear of the Lord will enter your heart. For you will reflect upon whence you came and whither you are going, and that even in your lifetime you are a worm and a maggot, how much more so after your death. And you will reflect that you will be called upon to give a full account of your deeds before the King of glory....
>
> I shall, therefore, explain to you how to conduct yourself with humility and how to make this virtue your own at all times. All your words should be spoken gently. Your head should be bent, your eyes gazing downward to the ground and your heart

> upward. When you address someone do not look him in the face. Let every man seem superior to you in your own eyes....
>
> Read this letter once a week and do not fail to keep its instructions.[10]

Anger makes us elevate ourselves over others in judgment. Nahmanides advises a number of techniques to assist in modifying anger, many of them involving body language suggesting submissiveness and subordination: bowing the head, lowering the eyes, imagining the heart advancing upwards, speaking softly. And then there are the larger conceptual ways that we humble ourselves: know from whence you came and before whom you are called in judgment. It is difficult to judge others when we imagine God judging us. When we think of the small space we will occupy in the ground at the end of our days, we begin to realize that we should carry ourselves with that smallness and humility while we are alive.

Maimonides also devised a technique to modify character problems – chief among them anger – for the life of the heart and mind. In this excerpt from the *The Laws of Character Traits,* Maimonides uses the Aristotelian notion of the golden mean to achieve balance in the face of anger or other character deficiencies:

> Each and every man possesses many character traits. Each trait is very different and distant from the others. One type of man is wrathful; he is constantly angry. [In contrast,] there is the calm individual who is never moved to anger, or, if at all, he will be slightly angry, [perhaps once] during a period of several years...[11]

> The two extremes of each trait, which are at a distance from one another, do not reflect a proper path. It is not fitting that a man should behave in accordance with these extremes or teach them to himself. If he finds that his nature leans towards one of the extremes or adapts itself easily to it, or, if he has learned one of the extremes and acts accordingly, he should bring himself back to what is proper and walk in the path of the good. This is the straight path.[12]

Although Maimonides generally advocates moderation, when it comes to anger, he believed that only yielding to humility in the extreme would help counter the problem.[13] When we suffer anger, Maimonides advises us to take on behavior that generates humility to pull ourselves to the opposite extreme, thereby locating an acceptable balance. The notion of achieving balance in this fashion may sound unrealistic but Jewish law is generally founded upon the notion that good deeds shape character. We do not wait for a generous impulse to give or to help others. That impulse may never surface, but if the world is built on kindness (Psalms 89:3) then enforced behaviors, witnessed and supported by communities of caring, help us manage our worst selves to bring out our best selves.

And if this method still sounds unlikely, we turn back the clock to 1897 to another Jewish writer: Max Beerbohm. Beerbohm wrote a story called "The Happy Hypocrite: A Fairy Tale for Tired Men," about a man named Lord George Hell. Lord George is not just mean; he also looks mean. He is cruel and depraved and seems beyond redemption. One day, Lord George sees a beautiful girl performing in a show. Her name is Jenny, and she is the essence of kindness. He falls deeply in love with her. But Jenny sees right through him, telling him that she would only marry a man with the face of a saint. Lord George begins to see himself through her eyes and realizes that he can never win Jenny's heart as he is. He develops a plan, asking a famous mask-maker in London to make him a saint's mask, one that will make him appear handsome and kind. This artisan is such an expert that no one can tell that Lord George is wearing a mask. Everyone believes that they are seeing Lord George's true new face. With this mask, Lord George approaches Jenny and eventually wins her heart. In registering their marriage, George writes his name as "George Heaven." Living with Jenny, he learns the art of selflessness and kindness. He is careful never to remove his mask, and he becomes a giving and wonderful husband to Jenny. Behind this mask, he has learned to become a different person, and he works hard to refrain from any of his former behaviors.

But the story does not end here. One day George encounters an old enemy; he had accumulated many in his previous life. The enemy sees straight through George's mask and, in front of Jenny, rips it off. Lord George is terrified – and the reader trembles in fear as well. But as the mask is ripped off, we find that George's face underneath is not the same face that it had been when he put the mask on. Over the years his features conformed to the mask and now – even underneath it – he is handsome and kind.

LIFE HOMEWORK

Consider the four types of anger: 1) quick to anger but quick to release it, 2) slow to anger but slow to release it, 3) slow to anger but quick to release it, and 4) quick to anger but slow to release it. Which most closely describes your temperament?

Once you have identified the category closest to your own type of anger, consider writing a letter to an imaginary someone (or to your children or life partner) that discusses the role anger plays in your life: in your childhood, perhaps on the receiving end of anger, and then as an adult. If you have children, think about their temperaments, how you help them with anger management, and the cost of anger in their relationships. In the letter, suggest techniques that might help someone in your anger category or another category handle anger in a more controlled, more helpful way.

PASSAGES FOR ADDITIONAL STUDY

Maimonides, *Mishneh Torah, The Laws of Repentance* 7:2

> A person should always view himself as leaning towards death, with the possibility that he might die at any time. Thus, he may be found as a sinner. Therefore, one should always repent from his sins immediately and should not say: "When I grow older, I will repent," for perhaps he will die before he grows older. This was implied by the wise counsel given by Solomon [Ecclesiastes 9:8]: "At all times, your clothes should be white."

Rabbi Moshe Haim Luzzatto, *The Path of the Just*, Chapter 6: "The Trait of Zeal"

> We see with our own eyes how often a person neglects his duty in spite of his awareness of it and in spite of his having come to recognize as a truth what is required for the salvation of his soul and what is incumbent upon him in respect to his Creator. This neglect is due not to an inadequate recognition of his duty nor to any other cause but the increasing weight of his laziness upon him; so that he says, "I will eat a little," or "I will sleep a little," or

"It is hard for me to leave the house"... and all the other excuses and pretenses that the mouth of fools is full of. Either way, the Torah is neglected, Divine service dispensed with, and the Creator abandoned.

Rabbi Abraham Isaac Kook, *The Lights of Repentance* 10:5

How wrongdoing dulls the intelligence, both the intelligence of the individual and the intelligence of society, of a generation and of an epoch! The divine word reaches a person from all its sources, from the Torah, from religious faith, from ancestral customs, from social mores, from his inner sense of equity – all these are channeled from the core reality in the spiritual order and its fullness, in the laws of heaven and earth, and their most basic essence. When degeneration leads him to embrace an outlook on life that negates his higher vision, then he becomes prey to the dark side within him, to his weaker self. The result is that he cannot muster the strength to hold on to the orderly structure of life as it makes its claims on him, whereby he is held back from sin and steered in the way of integrity as God fashioned him.

Text questions to think about while studying:

- How does thinking about one's death help manage anger?
- Laziness and anger have an unusual relationship to each other. How would you describe it?
- Why does anger hurt a higher vision of self?

Notes

1. For these midrashim in translation, see H.L. Strack and G. Stemberger, *Introduction to the Talmud and Midrash,* trans. M. Bockmuehl (Edinburgh: T&T Clark, 1991).
2. Rabbi Moshe Haim Luzzatto, *The Path of the Just* (Jerusalem: Feldheim Publishers, 1980), 161.
3. Shabbat 105b.
4. Luzzatto, *The Path of the Just,* 161.
5. Ibid.
6. Ibid., 163.
7. Ibid.
8. Ta'anit 20b.

9. Eiruvin 65b.
10. As translated by Louis Jacobs, *Jewish Ethics, Philosophy and Mysticism* (New York: Behrman House, 1969), pp. 19–21.
11. *Mishneh Torah, The Laws of Character Traits* 1:1–4.
12. *The Laws of Personality Development* 1:3.
13. Ibid., 2:3.

Day Eight

Joy

"For the sin we committed before You by callously hardening the heart."

This period of time often puts people in a somber mood. Reflecting on the self and the ways we need to change can easily slip into a depressive evaluation in which we always come up short, and when we do, the joy that is inherent in these holidays is lost, robbing us of the self-confidence we need to make the adjustments ahead.

One of the ways we capture the joy of this season is through music. Some of us regard the familiar tunes that have guided us in our prayers since childhood as a visit from old friends. The joy of singing in community and filling the sanctuary with haunting, ethereal tunes, some of which are over a thousand years old, carries us to a place of transcendence and loftiness. Even when the words dwell on judgment and consequences, the melodies lift us high above the content, inspiring us to live the lyrics and offering us the joyous possibility that anything can happen. We are united, strong, and beautiful. It is unadulterated spiritual happiness, and it is powerful.

One of the most joyous melodies of Yom Kippur is the song sung close to the end of the Musaf service praising the Kohen, high priest, who would enter the Holy of Holies and ask God to forgive us on Yom Kippur. If his sacrifice of expiation was not accepted, he died. If he left this holiest of chambers alive, the people rejoiced in ancient collective relief. They saw the Kohen's face lit with the majesty of forgiveness, a face that has become a model of the joy each of us experiences as we near the end of the service. We, too, have been forgiven. This song is often belted out in traditional congregations, as if we were standing and waiting in the Temple for our leader's appearance, and saw in our first glimpse of him the absolute happiness of a person exculpated from sin. The song focuses us on the serenity of this spiritual leader as he rejoined the people peacefully and unharmed. In the prayer, he is compared to a glitter of light, a rainbow in the clouds, a garment of splendor, a rose in a beautiful garden, a groom filled with grace, a bright star, an angel, a candle that shines in windows, the rising sun. As we raise our voices, we relive the moment of forgiveness with him. We are there. The moment is sweet and pure.

Since these songs are old friends, or new friends for some, it can be difficult when the person leading services picks an unfamiliar melody or one that you do not like. You feel betrayed since some of these prayers are only uttered once a year. You have to wait an entire year for another opportunity. As I have often said, "There is no anger like the anger at someone who does not sing your tunes." Not singing my tunes is like stealing my joy, and I have, on occasion, had the chutzpah to ask friends who lead services to repeat a prayer with my tune in the synagogue's coatroom since it just wouldn't be the holiday without hearing it.

In a High Holiday sermon, Rabbi Joseph Soloveitchik once observed that when he first arrived in Germany and heard Yom Kippur songs sung to joyful tunes, he was shocked; this was in stark contrast to his memory of services in Eastern Europe. Nevertheless, he observed that both approaches are legitimate, since "there is also great joy on the day that our sins are forgiven."[1] He experienced that joy in the act of fasting and reflected on how sad he would be if he were not able to fast. One of his great phobias was the fear that with age he might one day be forced to break the fast for medical reasons: "I do not fast because of any normative pressure. I simply find delight, joy, and happiness in fasting, praying, and cleansing myself."[2] The chance to start again from the inside out is a relief, a portal into lasting future happiness.

Sin and joy live in strange relation to each other. In Deuteronomy, we are remonstrated for not serving God with joy. Our happiness is a gift of faith, and if religion only makes us heavy-hearted and solemn then we have wronged it. "Because you did not serve the Lord, your God, with joyfulness and with gladness of heart by reason of the abundance of all things, therefore shall you serve your enemy whom the Lord shall send against you" (28:47–48). Maimonides cited this verse in his *Laws of Repentance* (9:1) as a proof-text that if you serve God with love you will experience great blessing, but the reverse is also true. In the same biblical book, God presents a pattern that repeats itself throughout our long and tortured history. Sin will remove you from your homeland and be the cause of your exile. During exile, you will begin to understand the cost of distance from God and pine for closeness. You will contemplate the causal relationship of actions and their consequences and pray to God and repent. God will then gather Israel "from all the peoples where the Lord your God has scattered you. Even if your outcasts are at the ends of the world" (30:3–4). The process of repentance on a national scale will make us stronger, and, as result, "He will make you more prosperous and numerous than your fathers" (30:5). The backsliding can be remedied. There is always a path out of sin, individual and collective, and that path back will yield more than one could have ever anticipated. It will bring happiness.

But the joy at the end of the long road home can be achieved, according to this text, only if there is recognition of sin, a self-awareness that we often create the worst of possible worlds for ourselves. In the prescription for a future of greater joy, God recommends an odd "medical" procedure, an opening of the heart; the term used in the verse literally means that God will circumcise our hearts. God will create a small hole, a puncture in the thickness of our stubborn, often callous hearts, so that we can experience true happiness and live: "Then the Lord your God will open up [*mal*] your heart and the hearts of your offspring to love the Lord your God with all your heart and soul, in order that you may live" (30:6). That small hole will release the blockage that gets in the way of authentic love and compassion. It is a spiritual stent, so to speak, that allows the heart to do its most important work.

Robert Goolrick, in his painful memoir, *The End of the World as We Know It*, writes about how much sorrow the human heart holds: "There is so much that happens to the human heart that is in the realm of the unthinkable, the unknowable, the unbearable."[3] We harden the heart so that nothing can get in, and for that we confess multiple times: "*For the sin we committed before You by callously hardening the heart.*" We make no hole for the release of unbearable pain. We hold it in, and it begins to warp our capacity for grace.

"The virtue of a sacred heart lies in the courage to maintain your innocence and wonder, your doubt and curiosity, and your compassion and love even through your darkest, most difficult moments."[4] This description of a sacred heart, a heart open to vulnerability and kindness, comes from an unexpected corner: a leadership book published by the Harvard Business School Press. In it, the authors observe that many leaders who develop thick skin to motivate and manage others harden themselves from the best of human nature and the transcendent and inspiring aspects of their work. But the message resonates far beyond the realms of leadership to that of everyday human experience. How can we keep the hole in our hearts open so that we can face life's vicissitudes and be appropriately touched by them without developing the callous outer layer that covers us and makes us numb to the range of human experience?

> A sacred heart means you may feel tortured and betrayed, powerless and hopeless, and yet you stay open. It's the capacity to encompass the entire range of your human experience without hardening or closing yourself. It means that even in the midst of disappointment and defeat, you remain connected to people and to the sources of your most profound purposes.[5]

Circumcision is not a word we usually associate with joy, and yet the idea of intentionally making oneself more vulnerable by removing an outer layer of protection is a lesson in how to live, in how to feel deeply. Our hearts need that hole. It must be wide enough to admit passion and compassion and anguish but small enough to filter the emotions that paralyze us, and prevent us from transformation and caring. This need and struggle is beautifully described in Rabbi Alan Lew's book about this season, *This Is Real and You Are Completely Unprepared*:

> Every soul needs to express itself. Every heart needs to crack itself open. Every one of us needs to move from anger to healing, from denial to consciousness, from boredom to renewal. These needs did not arise yesterday. They are among the most ancient of yearnings, and they are fully expressed in the pageantry and ritual of the Days of Awe, in the great journey we make between Rosh HaShana and Yom Kippur.[6]

Our ancient yearnings, our sincere desire to be forgiven, is so much more profound as an expression of joy than the petty happinesses society offers today as a meager excuse for joy: retail therapy, comfort food, medication, money, status, gossip.

Joy lies in sound judgment and goodness. In *Happiness in Premodern Judaism*, Hava Tirosh-Samuelson takes her readers through the Jewish classics, offering virtue as a Jewish synonym for joy and sprinkling that virtue with a good dose of wisdom. She takes us through a catalogue of psalms, noting that the very first psalm begins with the word "happy." Happiness is defined as virtue and wisdom from the outset: "Happy is the man who has not followed the counsel of the wicked or taken the path of sinners or joined the company of the insolent; rather the teaching of the Lord is his delight" (Psalms 1:1). The happy person keeps good company and delights in study. Excellence of character, she believes, is "a healthy departure from the relentless pursuit of material goods, wealth, power, and celebrity that characterizes much of our childish culture."[7] While virtue does not dispel pain or resolve every moral dilemma, it creates a noble and aspirational stretch and challenge for us. Imagine a society and culture that promotes excellence of character as the key to happiness. Judaism always has.

The positive psychologist and scholar Tal Ben-Shahar, in his book *Happier*, presents happiness through a range of personality types.[8] The nihilist believes neither in immediate happiness nor in long-term joy because all is ultimately vanity. The hedonist enjoys happiness now, knowing but usually ignoring the long-term consequences of his or her behavior. He may overeat, indulge in harmful sexual behavior, binge drink. Sometimes his short-lived impulses bring about almost tragic sadness. He drinks himself silly, disregarding the hangover that will, no doubt, appear the next day. Under the influence, he believes himself to be the captain of the universe, gets into a car, and hits and kills a pedestrian. His short-lived happiness brings untold despair to others.

We get a brief glimpse into such a moment in the Bible, when a wealthy man from the Carmel named Nabal slips up. David was not yet king. Protecting the area where Nabal lived, David sent some of his soldiers to get food from Nabal's estate. Nabal laughed off the request: "Who is David?" (1 Samuel 25:10). He spurned the request to give anything to these hungry soldiers, keeping it all for himself. When the soldiers passed on Nabal's message, David was incensed and ready to take up arms. Abigail, Nabal's wife, heard of the interaction and was mortified by her husband's behavior. She amassed food to feed them all and then personally traveled to greet David, before he arrived at her estate, and apologized for her husband with a clever play on words. A *naval* in Hebrew is a boor or a crass individual. "Please, my lord, pay no attention to that wretched fellow. For he is just what his name says. His name means 'boor' and he is a boor" (25:25). We admire her creativity but feel pity for this marriage.

When Abigail returns home, Nabal was enjoying a feast, hedonist that he was. The text points out the irony of his self-absorption, recording that he "made a feast fit for a king" but did not invite the future king who would one day reign over all of Israel. "Now Nabal was in a merry mood and very drunk," and Abigail was not able to tell him all that had transpired with David and how angry David was. "The next morning, when Nabal had slept off the wine, his wife told him everything that had happened; and his courage died within him, and he became like a stone" (25:37). David did not kill him. Nabal died a few days later from an unknown cause. His greed literally ate him to death.

Happier also presents the person most unlike the hedonist: she is on life's treadmill, finding herself in a rat-race for existence. She forfeits happiness now for future happiness, often securing neither. She hates her job but stays in it for the money and the dream of one day retiring to enjoy it all, not realizing that the "sunk happiness cost" – to adapt a concept from economics – may never pay off if the economy collapses or she becomes too unwell with age to enjoy all her past labors. People who forgo happiness today for a future happiness they can only imagine or aspire to are denying themselves the beauty of today without a guarantee for tomorrow.

Ben-Shahar proposes that the genuinely happy person does not live the life of the nihilist, the hedonist, or the ambitious person on the treadmill of monotony. A happy person for this positive psychologist is one who acts in a way that will make him feel good today and good tomorrow.

Maimonides, who occupies two chapters of Tirosh-Samuelson's *Happiness in Premodern Judaism,* promoted a return to virtue through repentance. In *The Guide of the Perplexed,* he reflects on the process of the heart cracking itself open and the seminal value of teshuva through an unusual word analysis. Maimonides comments more than once in his oeuvre on a very specific Hebrew word for randomness that appears seven times in the same chapter of Leviticus: "*keri,*" or chance. In Leviticus 26, a chapter on causality and the obligations of a covenantal relationship, God points to all the blessings that will accrue if we follow God's law, but then turns to the dangers of willful ignorance or outright hostility. Many translations take the word *keri* as a form of hostility or rejection. Maimonides prefers the notion of randomness or chance: you do not believe that events happen through divine providence but understand any tragedy as mere chance and, therefore, you neither learn to improve yourself nor seek meaning when bad things befall you. Without introspection, you will persist in this behavior, bringing only further distress upon yourself.

Maimonides identifies an additional problem with this thinking. The capacity for transformation always works in two directions. We slip up. We rebuild. We fall down. We pick ourselves up. Without meditating on wrongdoing or believing that repentance is possible, we allow our lives to move in only one direction: the spiral of descent.

> If then the individual believed that this fracture can never be remedied, he would persist in his error and sometimes perhaps

> disobey even more because of the fact that no stratagem remains at his disposal. If, however, he believes in repentance, he can correct himself and return to a better and more perfect state than the one he was in before he sinned.[9]

If there were no way back, then people would persist and even deepen their commitment to wrongdoing. Teshuva must exist in concept and in act to offer a road out of sin even before an act of sin is committed. The capacity to recalibrate and progress stands in relation to the gravitational pull downwards.

What happens to people who do not believe that repentance is a possibility? They shorten their joy. They cut themselves off from the liberation of the soul. As an illustration, we turn to the first penitent in the Bible: Cain. Cain killed his brother, committing the first murder between the very first brothers, not exactly a propitious beginning for the family dynamic moving forward. Only if we read Cain as an innocent who did not know the full freight of his anger or what the death of his brother really meant can we begin to understand how much Cain was tortured by his sin. Cain did not protest to God that his punishment was too great to bear, as many mistranslations render Genesis 4:13. The word "*avon*" is familiar in our prayers this season; it means sin, and once Cain understood that his brother would not return, he understood that he had to return. He had to rebuild his relationship with God and himself. He told God: "My sin is too great to bear." I cannot live with myself.

Sin strips us of joy. It traps and paralyzes us. It makes us restless and anxious. When sin is too great to bear, life stands in the balance.

God explained the primal surge of anger and our ability to overcome it before Cain killed Abel, but Cain did not understand it. "Why are you distressed, and why is your face fallen? Surely if you do right, there is uplift. But if you do not do right sin crouches at the door; its urge is towards you yet you can be its master" (4:6–7). Goodness lifts us up. Sin drags us down. Temptation appears every time we open the door, like a crouching animal ready to pounce. But we have mastery over the door. We can close it.

Cain did not heed these words. He opened the door to sin widely, and it pounced on him, egging him on, besetting him with its ferocity. The Italian Renaissance artist, Titian, rendered the murder as the tangle of muscular sinews; both brothers are locked in the tussle, but perhaps it was God's words that Cain ultimately wrestled with but could not conquer. The urge to do wrong is muscular and strong, virtually unyielding and persistent. But it can be defeated.

After the murder, when Cain reflected on the burden of his wrongdoing, he understood that in a world where primal urges reign, others could do to him what he did to his brother. He was terrified at the thought that he, too, could be murdered just as he had murdered. God gave him a mark of protection, and then Cain left the presence of God and married and had a child and built a city. Cursed with being a wanderer, Cain's repentance allowed him the stability to build a new life, to find joy.

Rabbi Mordechai of Lekhovitz (d. 1811), commenting on the verse about Cain's mark: "And the Lord set a sign for Cain lest anyone who meet him should kill him" (Genesis 4:15), observed that this odd sign upon Cain's forehead would be noticeable to all who saw him. That was precisely the point. His mark was a sign of preservation. The rebbe, however, did not regard it as a sign for others – but rather for Cain himself: "God gave Cain, the penitent, a sign of strength and holiness, so that no accident he met with should beat his spirit down and disturb him in his work of repentance."[10]

One midrash captures this happiness and the sadness of those for whom teshuva is elusive and hidden:[11]

> Adam met Cain and asked, "What was done in punishment of you?" Cain replied, "I vowed repentance and was granted forgiveness." Upon hearing this, Adam in self-reproach began to beat his face as he said, "Such is the power of repentance, and I knew it not." Then and there Adam exclaimed, "It is a good thing to confess to the Lord."[12]

Adam sinned and disobeyed God but since he never offered up his grief, he had no idea that teshuva was possible. He went down but could not go up. Repentance was not yet in the limited lexicon of human experience. It seems that repentance had to be discovered. It was neither instinctive nor assumed.

Rabbi Hanina ben Isaac, author of this midrash, added another dimension by excerpting a verse from elsewhere. What was Cain feeling when he left the presence of the Lord with this mark of protection? "He went forth rejoicing."

Forgiveness makes us happy. Goodness gives us life. Returning to moral clarity makes us whole again. Virtue lifts us up. Repentance brings us joy.

LIFE HOMEWORK

Think of three occasions this past year that were particularly joyful for you and why. If you are able to, write them down and contemplate why they made you happy. Did your joy have to do with material gain or the heightening of status or did it have to do with relationships, virtue, and goodness? Atomizing the ingredients of our personal happiness helps us recreate it in other situations. Too often we spend our emotional energies perseverating on what we did wrong and all of the consequences of wrongdoing. Sometimes we do this ourselves. At other times, people criticize us and analyze our faults. Today, spend some time analyzing your strengths and the sources of your happiness. How can you enhance your JQ – your joy quotient – in this coming year? Meaningful change happens from a place of confidence.

PASSAGES FOR ADDITIONAL STUDY

Maimonides, *Mishneh Torah, The Laws of Repentance* 8:6

There is no way in this world to grasp and comprehend the ultimate good which the soul will experience in the world to come. We only know bodily good and that is what we desire. However, that [ultimate] good is overwhelmingly great and cannot be compared to the good of this world except in a metaphoric sense. In truth, there is no way to compare the good of the soul in the world to come to the bodily goods of this world. Rather, that good is infinitely great, with no comparison or likeness. This is alluded to by David's statement [Psalms 31:20]: "How great is the good that You have hidden for those who fear You."

Rabbi Moshe Haim Luzzatto, *The Path of the Just*, Chapter 7: "Concerning the Divisions of Zeal"

It is to be observed that all of the deeds of the righteous are performed with alacrity. In relation to Abraham it is written, "And Abraham hastened to the tent, to Sarah, and he said, 'Hasten…' and he gave it to the youth and he hastened" (Genesis 18:6).

And in relation to Rebecca, "And she hastened and spilled her pitcher…" (Genesis 24:20). And in the midrash, "And the woman made haste…" (Bamdibar Rabba 10:17, Judges 13:10) – this teaches us that all the deeds of the righteous are done quickly, that they do not permit time to elapse before beginning them or completing them.

Rabbi Abraham Isaac Kook, *The Lights of Repentance* 16:8

Full penitence registers two seemingly contradictory effects on the soul: on the one hand anxiety and grief over the sins and the evil in oneself, and on the other hand confidence and satisfaction over the good, since it is impossible for the person not to discover some element of good in himself. Even if at times his assessment is confused and he cannot find anything good in himself, the very realization that sin and evil have produced in him anxiety and distress is itself of great merit. He should be happy, confident and full of vitality because of the measure of good. Thus even while seriously troubled by the emotion of penitence, he should be full of vitality, girded with the zeal for achievement and the joy of life and the readiness to experience its blessing.

Text questions to think about while studying:

- What is the source of ultimate joy in the texts above?
- How does speed in the performance of goodness demonstrate joy?
- Why does teshuva make the penitent happy and sad at the same time?

Notes

1. Aaron Rakeffet-Rothkoff, *The Rav: The World of Rabbi Joseph B. Soloveitchik* (New York: Ktav, 1999), 2:176. Also published in *Yemei Zikaron* (17:12): 240 (Yiddish).
2. Rakeffet-Rothkoff, *The Rav*, 2:177, from the Rav's lecture "Rashi on Aseret Hadibrot" at the RCA Annual Convention (June 30, 1970).
3. Robert Goolrick, *The End of the World as We Know It* (Chapel Hill: Algonquin Books, 2008), 95.

4. Ronald A. Heifetz and Marty Linsky, *Leadership on the Line* (Boston: Harvard Business School Press, 2002), 227.
5. Ibid., 230.
6. Alan Lew, *This Is Real and You Are Completely Unprepared* (Boston: Little, Brown and Co., 2003), 9.
7. Hava Tirosh-Samuelson, *Happiness in Premodern Judaism* (Cincinnati: Hebrew Union College Press, 2003), 449.
8. Tal Ben-Shahar, *Happier* (New York: McGraw-Hill, 2007).
9. Maimonides, *The Guide of the Perplexed* III:37, trans. Shlomo Pines (Chicago: University of Chicago Press, 1963), 2:540.
10. Martin Buber, *Tales of the Hasidim: Later Masters* (New York: Schocken Books, 1977), 155.
11. For more on this midrash and the topic, see Erica Brown, "Is Repentance Possible?" in *Confronting Scandal* (Woodstock, VT: Jewish Lights, 2010), 107–128.
12. *Genesis Rabba* 22:12.

Day Nine

Honesty

"For the sin we committed before You with verbal confession."

We are always apologizing. New research contends that most of us apologize about four times a week. We say sorry all of the time. Reading the findings might lead us to believe that as people we are honest, generally contrite, humble, able to confront our mistakes and also take accountability for them – until you read further; we actually apologize 22 percent more to strangers than to romantic partners and family.

And, contrary to popular opinion, men will apologize just as often as women if they feel they've done something wrong. Therein lies the discrepancy. Women tend to believe that they've done something wrong more often than men. Women also tend to get offended more easily than men. This means that women both say they're sorry and need others to apologize more often than men. In one study, 120 subjects imagined committing offenses, from being rude to a friend to inconveniencing another person they live with; researchers discovered that men apologized less frequently than women. The researchers concluded that men had a higher threshold for what they found offensive. "We don't think that women are too sensitive or that men are insensitive," says Karina Schumann, one of the study's authors. "We just know that women are more sensitive."[1]

This new research on the act of saying sorry also deals with the content of apologies and what people need to hear in order to grant sincere forgiveness. A "comprehensive" apology is more likely to win forgiveness, researchers say. According to a study conducted by the University of Waterloo, comprehensive apologies consist of eight elements:

- Remorse
- Acceptance of responsibility
- Admission of wrongdoing
- Acknowledgment of harm
- Promise to behave better
- Request for forgiveness
- Offer of repair
- Explanation

If any piece of this process is absent, it could compromise the acceptance of an apology. Sorry alone is not enough. Sorry without regret or admission of wrongdoing will not change the future. We may think that most people who hear us apologize do not want an explanation. "Just say sorry. I don't need to know why you did it." But what we are learning is that sorry without an explanation can leave the recipient feeling empty and unsatisfied. Sometimes when people hurt us, even inadvertently, they become an enigma to us. It can be hard to understand how and why someone acts differently than we would, especially when it comes to shameful, hurtful, or offensive behavior.

For this reason, the act of confession forces us to be more honest with ourselves *before* we apologize. This season requires difficult self-confrontation. We read words that may or may not force us to revisit the darker sides of self in search of clarity or to rebuild a relationship. By externalizing the words in confession, we begin to hear them differently and get insight into how someone else might hear and receive our words of forgiveness.

The language of confession we use in our prayerbooks is excerpted in part from the book of Daniel. Daniel realized that his people were suffering and that he had failed to be as brutally honest as necessary in his leadership:

> I turned my face to the Lord God, devoting myself to prayer and supplication, in fasting, in sackcloth and ashes. I prayed to the Lord my God, making confession thus: "O Lord, great and awesome God, who stays faithful to His covenant with those who love Him and keep His commandments! We have sinned; we have gone astray, we have acted wickedly; we have been rebellious and have deviated from Your commandments and Your rules, and have not obeyed Your servants the prophets who spoke in Your name to our kings, our officers, our fathers, and all the people of the land." (Daniel 9:3–6)

While the English may feel foreign, Daniel's Hebrew is painfully familiar:

חָטָאנוּ וְעָוִינוּ, הִרְשַׁעְנוּ וּמָרָדְנוּ; וְסוֹר מִמִּצְוֹתֶךָ, וּמִמִּשְׁפָּטֶיךָ.

This is the language that jumps off the pages of the *Maḥzor*, our High Holiday prayerbook, and into our most vulnerable places. It is the language of confession, and it is thousands of years old. Maimonides writes that confession is an elemental aspect of repentance, and repentance cannot be complete without it. Why not?

Confession is another word for naming. Instead of a personal problem resting in the cloud of words not articulated, confession forces us to put a name on an issue. Often naming a problem creates a path out of the problem. Those struggling with addiction in one of its many forms often cannot confess to the problem. The minute they can finally name it, they can begin to tackle it. Without a name, a problem will never be properly addressed. Without confession, there is no redemption. Rabbi Kook wrote that repentance actually begins the moment we commit a sin if we have an awareness of sin; the very recognition of an act of wrongdoing precipitates the beginning of teshuva, the road back to the self that is the emotionally and spiritually desired self.

Confession is a loaded English word that is not necessarily an accurate translation of the Hebrew word *vidui*. Naming, recognition, or acknowledgment may be more apt. In Deuteronomy, when Moses prepared the Israelites to enter the Promised Land, he told them that when they harvested their first fruits, they had to bring a basket of them to the Temple along with a verbal confession that begins with a brief history of our people. The history includes our most ancient ancestors, our servitude in Egypt, and the Exodus, and then finally our arrival in Israel and our new bounty. The food was to be left with God and then the person who brought it was to rejoice and "enjoy all the bounty that the Lord your God has bestowed upon you and your household" (26:11). This was a time of joy, not confession in its traditional, more oppressive sense. There is no confession of sin in this acknowledgment; merely a recognition, a naming, of all that has led up to this particular moment of gratitude. It is basket happiness – our joy is contained in something concrete that we are able to share with others.

The *vidui bikurim*, the name of this verbal offering, does review swaths of painful history. It mentions tribulations not worth repeating. And yet, each of those experiences must be mentioned because each went into the production and growth of every piece of fruit, as does every famine, rainfall, tragedy, and celebration. The pilgrimage would not have the same meaning, or the joy the same richness, if it all came easily. Confession helps us name all the parts of a process that lead up to a particular outcome.

Maimonides praised those who confessed in public, who had the courage to denounce personal wrongdoing to others.[2] This was regarded as a higher level of commitment to teshuva precisely because exposing our weaknesses forces others to become witnesses to our transformation. But Maimonides also made a distinction between public confession of sins between human beings and sins between a person and God. In the latter category, he writes: "But sins between man and God should not be made public, and he is brazen-faced if he does so."[3] Public confession assumes a greater level of honesty unless it is about a public performance. No sincerity required. When confession acts as false piety it fails the lie detector test.

In his master work, *On Repentance*, Rabbi Joseph Soloveitchik pondered Maimonides' distinction between confession to God and fellow humans: "At times, a man may confess and declare his sins as a means of winning public approval, so that others will admire him and say, 'what a righteous man he is!'.... What the public thinks of him cannot matter when he stands 'before God, blessed be He.'"[4] If honesty is what we are ultimately seeking, then confession can be confession only if it provokes truth, not if it masks lies.

Facing the truth rather than masking a lie takes us to the bed of a virile King David, crippled by the news that the child born of his illicit relationship with Bathsheba was ill to the point of death. The chapter that relays the narrative begins with the ominous words: "But the Lord was displeased with what David had done" (II Samuel 12:1). Nathan the prophet offered David a parable to help the king understand how wrong his affair with Bathsheba had been, a tale of sordid adultery, murder, and deception. Through the subtlety of Nathan's parable, David was able to loosen his defenses and confess: "I stand guilty before the Lord" (12:13). David was able to hear Nathan because the prophet's creative framework did not let David escape from confrontation with sin. Nathan added another dimension to his chastisement. He helped this confused king understand that he had overreached, that he had been blessed with so much that his greedy desire for this woman should have been curbed by his already overflowing bounty. Nathan expressed it as if from God's very mouth:

> It was I who anointed you king over Israel and it was I who rescued you from the hand of Saul. I gave you your master's house and possession of your master's wives; and I gave you the house of Israel and Judah and if that were not enough, I would give you twice as much. Why then have you flouted the command of the Lord and done what displeases Him? (12:7–9)

God gave David everything: power, prestige, and intelligence. Did David not have enough that he needed more, another man's wife? Since David arranged for Uriah, Bathsheba's husband, to be killed by the sword, he would suffer the sword's ugliest wounds himself: "Therefore the sword shall never depart from your house.... I will make a calamity rise against you from within your own house" (12:10–11).

God's words implied a military upheaval in the future, but God made no mention of the battlefield, the place of David's many successes. David had approached Goliath with stones; his physical strength and military acumen were well-known by this point in his story. The battles David could not win were those that touched his own home life.

Nathan pronounced the punishment: "The child about to be born to you shall die" (12:14). After Nathan left the royal palace, the child became critically ill. David prayed and fasted. His servants tried to feed him, but he refused. A week after Nathan left, the child died, but David's servants were too afraid to tell him. Since David had not listened to their adjurations to eat, they were certain he would not accept the bad news, that he would do something terrible. They were wrong. David saw the servants speaking in whispers to each other and then he understood what had happened. He forced them to be honest:

> "Is the child dead?"
> "Yes."

We hear the anguish of the question and the anguish of the answer. There was no room for grey. Honesty stood starkly and painfully alone.

David washed and changed his clothes, went to pray, and then asked for a meal. The servants were again confused. How was it that their king rejected all food when this infant was sick but once the child died, he was able to eat? David responded with clarity. When the child was ill, perhaps there was still some small hope for compassion. But once the boy was dead, David knew that he had to face the brutal truth: "Now that the child is dead, why should I fast? Can I bring him back again? I shall go to him, but he shall never come back to me" (12:23).

The truth hurts. It hurts more than any lie we could tell ourselves. But the truth is not going away.

King Solomon saw this stubborn tendency when he finished building the First Temple and contemplated whether or not God could ever be limited to any space. King Solomon understood the function that the building might one day have far into the future, describing life not in the land of Israel but in the Diaspora at the hand of enemies. The Temple would then have a different function; it would become a holy space, only aspirational in nature, precisely because the pattern of sin and forgiveness is predictable:

> When they sin against You – for there is no man who does not sin – and You are angry with them and deliver them to the enemy, and their captors carry them off to an enemy land, near or far, and they take it to heart in the land to which they have been carried off, and they repent and make supplication to You in the land of their captors, saying: "We have sinned, we have acted perversely, we have acted wickedly," and they turn back to You with all their heart and soul, in the land of the enemies who have carried them off, and they pray to You in the direction of their land which You gave to their fathers, of the city which You have chosen, and of the house which I have built to Your name – give heed in Your heavenly abode to their prayer and supplication, uphold their cause, and pardon Your people who have sinned against You for all the transgressions that they have committed against You. Grant them mercy. (1 Kings 8:46–50)[5]

We turn our hearts away. We sin. We suffer. We turn our hearts towards. God hears. God redeems. We turn our hearts away.... King Solomon offers an ancient theological equivalent of "lather, rinse, repeat." It happened before. It will happen again. And again.

As a result, we often hear an apology and judge it as insincere or simply false. It does not sound like the truth. After all, we apologize for a lot of reasons that have nothing to do with the truth: to get out of trouble, because it is expected, to end an argument, out of politeness, to repair a relationship, to move on. These are all valid reasons but are not honest responses; when we apologize for any of these reasons, we are not necessarily engaging in a serious reckoning on a specific problem. Just watch the way people ask for forgiveness in Jewish settings about this time of the year. I distinctly remember in high school the day before Yom Kippur, we would walk down the halls asking anyone and everyone for *meḥila*, for forgiveness, with spitfire speed but with hardly a moment for any authentic response. We never anticipated someone turning around and saying, "Actually, you really hurt me this past year."

We waited for the hasty "yes" and for the question to be reciprocated at a fast enough pace to allow us to move on to someone else. The apology is regarded as the formal pass that lets us continue or progress. It's not about process; it's about a shallow fulfillment of a legal requirement. It's not about truth; it's about peace.

And we even force-feed this peace to ourselves, instead of confronting the truth, with a nightly prayer before going to sleep. We grant forgiveness to everyone who may have insulted us intentionally or unintentionally, even though they may have no idea that we are nursing a wound:

> Master of the Universe, I forgive anyone who angered or troubled me or wronged me, whether to my person, my finances, my dignity or any other offense – whether it was done under coercion or done as an act of will, accidentally or intentionally, with words or with actions, in this life or another. [I extend this forgiveness] to any individual and ask that no one be punished on my account. May it be Your will, My Lord, God and the God of my ancestors that I will sin no more nor return to those ways, neither will I anger You nor do anything bad in Your eyes. May the wrongs that I have done be erased by Your infinite compassion but not through suffering or sickness. May the words of my heart find favor before You, God, My Rock and Redeemer.

Rabbi Israel Meir Kagan, the Hafetz Hayim, wrote in his legal commentary – composed at the turn of the twentieth century – that the daily recitation of this prayer could extend one's life. Perhaps he did not mean it as a medical guarantee but rather as an observation about what cuts life short. The stress of lying in bed stewing over an insult or patching a bruised ego can shorten one's life, if not in actual duration then in quality. Pick truth or pick peace. You can have one, but you cannot have both.

Truth or peace.

Because our apologies are not always real apologies, we find ourselves visiting and revisiting familiar problems. Every year, we find ourselves asking forgiveness from the same people for the same offenses. Every year, we recommit ourselves to work on the same self-improvement projects we've pledged ten times before. Every year, on wedding anniversaries, we celebrate the number of years we have had the same argument. Is it any wonder that we confess to empty confessions every Yom Kippur? "For the sin we committed before You with verbal confession."

Truth (*emet*) and peace (*shalom*) rarely live together compatibly. You can be honest or you can love people. Any uncomfortable mix of both will usually involve compromising one of these two priorities. We find this oddly demonstrated in one of the most moving prayers of these Days of Awe. Towards the end of "*Hineni*" – the prayer said by the cantor or prayer leader before the Musaf service – we find truth and peace in a happy marriage: "May they love truth and peace, and may there be no impediment in my prayer." If you know Hebrew grammar you can appreciate that the tenses are not properly aligned, and if you are a student of the Hebrew Bible, you may recognize the first clause of this sentence from the book of Zechariah (8:19). A more precise translation renders the expression differently: "You must love honesty and integrity."

Our prayer leader is telling us that we must love honesty and integrity in order to pray with sincerity and that he hopes his prayers will be heard and accepted on behalf of the community. We have a job to do, and he has a job to do.

The chapter from which this clause is excerpted is about exile and redemption and the fasts that mark the destruction of Jerusalem. Zechariah told the Israelites that these fast days would one day turn into times of happiness, with the tail admonition: You must love honesty and integrity. Some medieval commentaries regard the clause as conditional. If you are honest and upright, God will uphold his promises. Abraham ibn Ezra (d. 1167) is more radical in his interpretation. He regards the repetition of fasting as a form of questioning posed to the prophet: do we have to fast again and again? To this Zechariah answers, "If you are honest and a person of integrity you will never have to fast again. All the fast days will be turned into days of celebration."

The combination of *emet* and *shalom* is not unusual in the Bible, and is even repeated in the same chapter of Zechariah. It also appears in the very last verse of the book of Esther. But no matter how often the values are placed side-by-side, they always live in dialectic tension.

Truth is usually uncompromising, rigid, just, hard, and unyielding. We see peace as a value because it is compromising, bendable, negotiable, flexible, even resigned at times. These two values cannot live together. You cannot be compromising and uncompromising at the same time. How can God demand that we love two acts or traits or ways of being that cannot coexist? Ralph Waldo Emerson once wrote, "No man speaks the truth or lives a true life two minutes together."[6] Perhaps the cantor asks something of us that he knows we can never deliver. It might be easier to sing while fasting than for us to live with our assignment.

This dichotomy is the basis of many famous works of literature, from Victor Hugo to Herman Melville to Nathaniel Hawthorne. People hold up one act of injustice, one stolen loaf of bread, one crime, and can never forgive it, despite other acts of kindness or a general context of goodness. Even in the face of profound repentance, those who love narrow justice believe that every wrongdoing mounts against us.

But we do not have to look to literature to show us the uneasiness of these values in confrontation with each other. Every day we are faced with a media barrage of truth in battle with peace. Fundamentalists the world over believe that there is truth with a capital "T" and cannot make peace. They are unable to see beyond their own reality and recognize the reality of another. Protracted political battles ensue over these values. Lives are lost because we are unable to make sense of these three Hebrew words, *"Ha'emet v'hashalom ehavu,"* in the *"Hineni"* prayer.

We may gain clarity on the relationship of truth and peace from another verse in Zechariah where these values also appear: "These are the things you are to do: speak the truth to one another, render true and perfect justice in your gates" (9:16). The French medieval exegete Rabbi David Kimhe, known as the Radak, explained that one should avoid saying one thing with the heart and another with the mouth, and that if one judges with integrity, one will create peace. Rashi interpreted this to mean that one must say what must be said privately but judge transparently. A later commentator, Rabbi David Altshuler, the *Metzudat David,* commenting on Zechariah 9:16, warned: "When you corrupt justice, you create neither truth nor peace."

Literature sustains tension to retain interest, so we find peace versus truth as a leitmotif in many fine novels. But in life, our responsibility is to minimize tensions and not to pit values against each other, which can cause grave confusion and confound judgment. People of integrity have to know, as the prophet Zechariah advised, when to be flexible and when to be inflexible, when to compromise and when to stand on principle, when to hold back and when to hold forth. And they must know when a commitment to too much honesty may cause strife and despair. Kahlil Gibran (1883–1931), the Lebanese-American poet, said: "Say not that I have found *the* truth but rather, 'I have found *a* truth.'"[7]

We cannot embody truth over peace, one value over another. We must profoundly love both, even if circumstances ask for one response over another at times. That is why it is so hard to ask for forgiveness. And that is why it is so hard to grant forgiveness.

The cantor works hard on these days, but he also has it easy. The cantor must ask God to listen to prayers on our behalf. We, on the other hand, have to be worthy of them. We have to love truth and peace and hold them in proper balance. The cantor sings it for us so that we may live it. And by putting two contradictory impulses next to each other and forcing them into a relationship, we are asked to contemplate Walt Whitman's confounding statement in *Song of Myself*: "Do I contradict myself? Very well, then, I contradict myself. I am large, I contain multitudes." We cannot love peace and truth in equal measure all of the time, but we understand on these holiest of days that honesty consists of holding them both in our hands when we make judgments; we contain multitudes. If we ask, every day of these ten days, that God balance truth and peace, justice and mercy, on the divine scale when judging us, we, too, must learn how to balance the scales.

Honesty lies somewhere between truth and peace. Wisdom demands that we face difficult truths, but also that we cushion truths when their brutality obstructs our relationships or our attempts at self-improvement. Peace, too, must prevail in our far-from-ideal world. It, too, has an important place in the realm of honesty. "God protects the honest," Psalms tells us (31:24). We enjoy divine protection when we strive to balance two foundational values of our tradition. Let honesty be our hallmark.

LIFE HOMEWORK

Exercise 1:

Can you hold truth and peace in a loving relationship with each other? This year, as you review your parenting, consider whether you have achieved the proper balance between being compromising and uncompromising with your children? Have you done so with your spouse, your parents, your friends? At school or at work, have you known when to stand on principle and when to let go, when to be harsh and critical and when to show compassion? Have you been too harsh on yourself or not harsh enough? Have you faced truths about your faults or made a too-easy peace with them?

Exercise 2:

In our house, at the meal before Yom Kippur starts, everyone receives the questions below on a sheet of paper. After writing the answers, each person at the table receives an envelope containing all of the answers to the same questions from previous years. We read them to ourselves and then deposit our new sheet and our old ones in an envelope and date it. The envelopes keep getting bigger. Sometimes we realize that we have been able to meet challenges that we had identified in the past. At other times, we find ourselves repeating the same transgressions or working on the same relationship year after year. Feel free to use these questions at your table or review them in your mind. The idea is to take small steps, to move teshuva from impossibility to possibility, to be as honest as possible:

- Think of one person you have hurt this year. How can you fix it?
- What is one small and realistic thing you can do to make yourself a better person this year?
- What can you do this year to be a better student or professional?
- What is one thing you really want to pray for this year?
- What is one thing you can do to strengthen your relationship with God this year?

PASSAGES FOR ADDITIONAL STUDY

Maimonides, *Mishneh Torah, The Laws of Repentance* 9:1

We are promised by the Torah that if we fulfill it with joy and good spirit and meditate on its wisdom at all times, [God] will remove all the obstacles that prevent us from fulfilling it, for example, sickness, war, famine and the like. Similarly, He will grant us all the good that will reinforce our performance of the Torah, such as plenty, peace, an abundance of silver and gold in order that we not be involved throughout all our days in matters required by the body, but rather, will sit unburdened and [thus, have the opportunity to] study wisdom and perform mitzvot in order that we will merit the life of the world to come.

Rabbi Moshe Haim Luzzatto, *The Path of the Just*, Chapter 11: "The Particulars of Cleanliness"

Lying is a terrible illness that has spread far-reaching among men. There are various levels of this sin. There are some whose profession itself is lying, who go around inventing stark falsehoods in order to promote social intercourse or to be reckoned among the wise and informed. In relation to them it is said (Proverbs 12:22) "The abomination of God is lying lips," and (Isaiah 59:3) "Your lips speak falsehood, your tongues give voice to wrong."

Rabbi Abraham Isaac Kook, *The Lights of Repentance* 13:9

The inner moral sense calls out to man: Son of man, turn back from your sins! Sometimes the call is so loud that it disturbs all the harmonious balance of life. A person must then rise to a higher spiritual standard in order to stabilize his inner world, but here he will need the help of courage. A person's inner courage must come to his aid when he goes through the most serious spiritual crisis.

Text questions to think about while studying:

- What is the ideal picture of life created in the texts above?
- What are the obstacles that get in the way of human perfection?
- How does dishonesty behave as an obstruction to the life of goodness?

Notes

1. See Elizabeth Bernstein's article, which cites the studies "I'm Very, Very, Very Sorry... Really?" in the *Wall Street Journal,* Oct. 18, 2010, http://online.wsj.com/article/SB10001424052702304410504575560093884004442.html.
2. Maimonides, *Mishneh Torah, The Laws of Repentance* 2:5.
3. Ibid.
4. Rabbi Joseph Soloveitchik, *On Repentance* (Jerusalem: Oroth Publishing House, 1980), 89.
5. I am grateful to my husband for this observation.
6. Ralph Waldo Emerson, *The Journals and Miscellaneous Notebooks of Ralph Waldo Emerson: 1835–1838* (Cambridge, MA: Belknap Press of Harvard University Press, 1965), 22. Also available online at http://archive.org/stream/cu31924021990217/cu31924021990217_djvu.txt.
7. Kahlil Gibran, *The Prophet* (New York: Alfred Knopf, 1923), 54.

Day Ten

Holiness

"For the sin we committed before You by desecrating the Divine Name."

"You shall be holy, for I, the Lord your God, am holy" (Leviticus 19:2). Holiness is a mandate. We are obligated to be holy but without necessarily understanding what holiness demands of us. The German theologian Rudolph Otto (1869–1937) tried to analyze the component parts of the sacred in his book *The Idea of the Holy*, but Otto's language is dense and opaque.[1] Holiness, Otto believed, is a mystery, both terrifying and fascinating. He believed that holiness is a non-rational and non-sensory experience that he termed "numinous," referring to its unknowable quality. As interesting and influential as Otto's writing is, the book offers little practical guidance on what it could mean to live the lofty and ethereal demands of this call from Leviticus.

As we become more attuned to the sacredness of each day of the ten days of repentance, we confess when we have fallen short of this desideratum. Further on in Leviticus, sanctifying God and profaning

God live right next to each other: "You shall not profane My holy name, that I may be sanctified in the midst of the Israelite people, I the Lord who sanctify you" (22:32). The verse presents what looks like a causal relationship. If I do not profane, then I sanctify. But holiness does not strike us as a neutral state that demands no active striving. We wonder what it means to desecrate God's name just as we try to understand what it means to make it holy in our act of *vidui*, confession. Is desecration a conscious act of minimizing God's presence in our lives or even profaning it, or is it simply ignoring the sacred, pretending that transcendence is not relevant to us? A midrash on the book of Numbers hints at the second:

> Entrances to holiness are everywhere.
> The possibility of ascent is all the time.
> Even at unlikely times and through unlikely places.
> There is no place on earth without the Presence.[2]

There are portals to holiness everywhere, but we often walk in the world as if we have no map to them, as if they do not exist. Rabbi Lawrence Kushner's interpretation of this midrash prods us to ask if we really strive for holiness on this day and every day after it:

> You do not have to go anywhere to raise yourself. You do not have to become anyone other than yourself to find entrances. You are already there. You are already everything you need to be. Entrances are everywhere and all the time. "There is no man who does not have his hour, and no thing that does not have its place" (*Ethics of the Fathers* 4:3).[3]

As we move up the ladder of holiness on Yom Kippur, we realize that we have scaled the heights to arrive at this entrance but feel lower than ever before. We cannot access a way in to God. We gravitate between intimacy and distance. One minute we are close to imbuing everything we do with transcendence and the next we feel all of our inadequacies rising, filling us with dread and humility.

Our prayer moments parallel this experience, taking us up and down with their ascents and descents, mirroring this emotional rise and fall with uncanny unpredictability. We praise God's name and God's capacity for mercy, elevating us and giving us the promise to reach out and bridge the chasm. Then suddenly our prayers turn precipitously to human beings and throw us into existential crisis:

> Man, his beginning is from dust and ends in dust; risking his life, he gets his bread. He is like a potsherd that cracks, like grass that withers, like the flower that fades, like the shadow that passes, like the cloud that vanishes, like the wind that blows, like the dust that flies, and like a fleeting dream... (*Unetaneh Tokef* prayer)

The impermanence of our condition renders our grasp for the sacred an anomaly. We are here and then we will go, sometimes without notice. We have the same ephemeral quality as shadows, dust, and dreams. We cannot achieve the sacred; we are as breakable as clay. And again, as we immerse ourselves in these doubts and anxieties, the prayer mood shifts again: "But You are the King, the Almighty, the living and the everlasting God." Our frailty is contrasted to God's stability, and we find ourselves once again on terra firma. We will hold on tightly to the Rock and gain strength from God's presence.

To be holy in Hebrew is to consecrate or separate something so that it achieves distinction. We step out of our this-worldly experience and into another, one which exudes mystery and strangeness. When Moses experienced revelation at the burning bush, God told him to remove his shoes, to take off his layer of this-worldliness so that he could enter another universe of discourse. He had to take off that which separated him from the ground to understand that he was not in a place ruled by expected norms: "Remove your sandals from your feet, for the place on which you stand is holy ground" (Exodus 3:5). When Moses was called he answered, "*Hineni.*" I am in the moment. I am fully present. I have answered the call to holiness. Only in that state will the impossible become possible.

We are standing right now, at this moment in time, on the brink of infinite possibility. We stand here as individuals ready for change, enveloped and carried by the love of community. There are no divisions. There are no distractions. As we enter this, the holiest day of the year, we are saying with the setting of the sun that we have let go of the insistence that all is impossible, all the thoughts and intentions and motivations that tell us we can never change. For the next twenty-five hours, we will separate ourselves from this world in order to experience another world where all change is possible. The doors to possibility are opening. They are waiting for us to say *hineni*: I am fully present here, and I can achieve the impossible.

But what if you are not ready to say *hineni* to the call of holiness as Moses did? What if you do not believe that people can really change or that the portals into transcendence are really accessible? The possibility of teshuva has been argued for millennia. You are not alone.

We begin with the argument for impossibility. Teshuva undoubtedly is an impossible idea. It asks us to believe without question that people can change. This represents an enormous leap of faith for most. There are people who can believe in an intangible God, but the same individuals cannot believe that they can change themselves. Better yet, there are those who believe that they can change but that no one else can: "He'll always be the same." "Once an addict, always an addict." "She always does that."

And then we turn to the ultimate story of the impossibility of teshuva. It is told in any number of places, from passages in the Talmud to Milton Steinberg's *As a Driven Leaf*.[4] In Ḥagiga 15a, we find one of the Talmud's most colorful characters: Elisha ben Abuya, the grade A heretic of an ancient past whose name was changed to "Aḥer" – or the Other – when he became a heretic. He was once a learned scholar but then became someone else, a person who had lost his faith. He witnessed a young boy obeying the command of his father to climb a tree and shoo away a mother bird to retrieve its eggs. The lad fulfilled two biblical commandments, the only two that promise long life, but toppled off the tree and died. In wonder, Elisha ben Abuya, who witnessed the fall, responded in disbelief: "Is this the Torah, and is this its reward?" and then dropped his faith.

Rabbi Meir, Aḥer's most devoted student, studied Torah with

him even when he left traditional Judaism. The Talmud tells us of a time when the two were traveling together on Shabbat. A lengthy *Tosafot*, medieval commentary, on this story uses one version to suggest that it was not on just any Shabbat but Shabbat and Yom Kippur at the same time. It was the second half of the first century on a day of holiness with the added bonus of being even more holy than usual. Rabbi Meir was walking and learning from Aḥer, who was riding a horse on the Shabbat of Yom Kippur, transgressing a well-known prohibition. The scene itself seems unimaginable. They reached the *teḥum Shabbat*, the invisible boundary beyond which carrying is no longer permitted, and Aḥer told Rabbi Meir to go back. He did not want to be responsible for the violations of his student, whose faith remained intact. Rabbi Meir, using the notion of this boundary as a metaphor for change, said to his revered teacher, the heretic, "You also turn back." The words were few but loaded. Turn away from crossing this red line with me and repent. Come home. And Elisha uttered the ultimate statement of impossibility: "Haven't I already told you that I heard from behind the curtain, 'Return my wayward children, all, that is, except for Aḥer'?"

Aḥer used the perfect justification. He had, he claimed, heard God tell him directly ("behind the curtain" is a talmudic metaphor for veiled divine knowledge) that everyone has the possibility of changing but him. In this act of gross self-justification, he turned the very principles he once lived by upside down, believing that he was the only exception to the rule.

When we read this talmudic legend, we believe Aḥer. We take his words at face value. Perhaps some metaphysical voice did call and tell him that everyone has a chance to change, everyone but him. Rabbi Jonathan Sacks, my own revered teacher, once explained that Aḥer's convincing himself that everyone could change but him was an act of great denial. If everyone has the capacity to be different, then there are no exceptions to the rule. It cannot be possible for everyone but impossible for him. Aḥer's denial was so profound that he convinced himself and tried to convince Rabbi Meir that God Himself would reject Aḥer's repentance.

Someone who already made enormous changes in his own life should have been the first to understand that change is always possible.

But for him, change was only in one direction. Aḥer may have spoken about himself in the third person in this passage in order to distance himself from the message. Had he used his own given name, perhaps he would never have had the gumption to make such a statement, one that flew in the face of everything he knew about his God, his former faith, and his understanding of teshuva. Elisha separated some part of himself from what he knew to be a deep truth and spoke in the name of a God he rejected, falsifying God's word and God's promise. He convinced himself that change is impossible.

In a similar vein, the Jerusalem Talmud records an odd conversation about the possibility of change in contrast to Aḥer's limited view. The question the Talmud presents is simple: What is a sinner's punishment? Piecing together and then weaving verses liberally for answers, a common stylistic feature of *aggada* (rabbinic legends), the question is answered by wisdom, the prophet, the Torah, and God:

> Wisdom was asked, "What should be the punishment for the sinner?" She answered, "Let evil pursue the sinner."
>
> Prophecy was asked, "What should be the punishment for the sinner?" She answered, "The soul that sins shall perish."
>
> The Torah was asked, "What should be the punishment for the sinner?" She answered, "Let him bring a sacrifice, and be atoned for."
>
> The Holy One, Blessed be He, was asked, "What should be the punishment for the sinner?" He answered, "Let the sinner repent, and he will find atonement."[5]

Wisdom here uses the voice of common sense. Common sense understands that when a person sins, he or she will suffer consequences. Sin will become its own punishment because an individual will have to live with the fact of sin in his or her life. Sin also promotes more sin, with its tumble-down effect captured in the aphorism: "Sin generates sin" in *Ethics of the Fathers* (4:2).

Prophecy takes a larger emotional view of sin's impact. Each sin can be eliminated through punishment or recompense but, in the aggregate, sin has a corrosive effect. It wears us down. It changes us. It rusts our commitments.

The Torah takes a legal view and looks at what is technically demanded of us when we commit particular sins. We have to then make sacrifices so that God will grant atonement. If you bring a sacrifice the impact of sin is voided. In each instance an act must be done to eliminate the after-effects of sin.

The dichotomy between the prophet's response and the Torah's response is beautifully played out in an observation Rabbi Joseph Soloveitchik makes in *On Repentance*. Does teshuva imply some level of continuity of the past or the cutting off of the past? When the prophet speaks of the corrosion of the soul, he understands that the soul is the same soul, layered now with the imprint of sin. The Torah's understanding is that a sacrifice nullifies the past; it is as if the sin had never been committed.

> The question whether repentance implies continuity or severance, whether it sustains the past or utterly nullifies it, depends upon the nature of the repentance. There is repentance which does allow for continuity and which accords recognition to the past, and there is also repentance whose goal is the utter annihilation of the evil in the soul of man. Certain situations leave no choice but for the annihilation of evil and for completely uprooting it.[6]

The punishment mentioned in the question is not really punishment at all. What the Talmud is searching for is a deeper understanding of the consequence of sin. Sin leads to more sin. Sin weakens our resistance and corrupts. Sin is finite and transactional. It can be totally removed with the proper payment. Every one of these other lodestones of Jewish life teaches that when we transgress there is a cost attached.

Rabbi Simha Bunim, the Hasidic sage, once asked his students how they could tell when a sin had been pardoned in an age without prophets. His students struggled to come up with an answer but none satisfied the rebbe. "We can tell," he responded, "by the fact that we no longer commit that sin."[7]

Into this lively discussion comes the last and most authoritative voice: God's. God offers a response far and away the most conceptual and difficult to grasp. A sinner must repent. Ultimately that is all that is required. God defies the limitations of the other positions and says, "Just change." No punishment, no rusting of the soul, no sacrifice will mean more to the future of the individual than the capacity and willingness to change. When that is present, God accepts repentance wholesale.

At its very core, this piece of *aggada* assumes that teshuva defies common sense, intellectual reasoning, legal manipulation, and even prophetic wisdom – for how can one undo what was? Quite simply. Teshuva is a divine gift. It makes the impossible possible. Finally, a cryptic piece of Talmud now becomes somewhat clearer:

> Seven things were created before the world was created.... The Torah, repentance, the Garden of Eden, Gehenna, the Throne of Glory, the Temple, and the name of the Messiah.... Repentance, for it is written, "Before the mountains were brought forth" (Psalms 90:2).[8]

"Before the mountains were brought forth" implies that there were places and concepts created before the world was created because they defy rationality; they represent something that could not belong to a world governed by natural law. Teshuva defies reason. But, nevertheless, it exists.

The moment you shift from the impossible to the possible, you create the possibility of doing that which seems impossible. And we, as Jews, are tied into an historic nation that has defied all odds and every rational force against it. We are the people of impossibility. David Ben-Gurion said in considering the impossibility of the State of Israel, "Anyone who does not believe in miracles is not a realist." Our national anthem, *Hatikva,* is about a hope unseen and unimaginable. And what is teshuva, after all, but the most personal of miracles, the miracle of accepting and shaping a new self?

The German psychologist Kurt Lewin (1890–1947) once wrote: "If you want to truly understand something, try to change it." Lewin escaped World War II by moving to the United States in the early 1930s, and after visiting professorships in a number of universities, directed the Center for Group Dynamics at MIT. He achieved fame because he believed that "human behavior is the function of both the person and the environment." In other words, human behavior is related to both personal characteristics and the social situations in which we find ourselves. This may not seem new to us, but it was radical when he introduced it. Lewin's research also implied that change is imminently possible. Adaptation, evolution, adjustment: these are all words that imply a new configuration to an already existing model of behavior. Tweaking something also changes it. Radical transformation is not always necessary or desirable; it can make teshuva seem harder than it has to be. Lewin understood that if you want to get to know someone or something, you need to change it. That process will bring forth resistance, curiosity, rigidity, or willingness. Change is stubborn, but it happens.

John Kotter, in *The Heart of Change*, writes: "People change what they do less because they are given analysis that shifts their thinking than because they are shown a truth that influences their feelings."[9] In other words, the heart of change is in the emotions; it is not about the pros and cons of any given decision. It transcends that. When it comes to teshuva, we may be trying to influence one side of the brain that resists us and makes it seem that repentance is out of bounds, when another side of our brain might be more receptive.

In Ezekiel, God tells us that He will help us with the daunting task of becoming holy. He will sprinkle cleansing waters upon us, removing the aura of sin that trails us at times: "And I will give you a new heart and put a new spirit into you. I will remove the heart of stone from your body and give you a heart of flesh, and I will put My spirit into you" (36:25–26). We walk into the last prayers of the day, *Ne'ila*, almost cleansed of sin, with a new heart and a new spirit. Holiness is very close to us right now.

Rabbi Kook wrote poetry and, just as he wrote that repentance is a great theme for poets and painters, his poem "Remove My Shame" moves us from sin to holiness, from Ezekiel's transgression to a new heart and a new spirit:

> Remove my shame,
> Lift my anxiety,
> Absolve me of my sin
> And enable me to pray before You
> With gladness of heart,
> To pursue Your commandments and Your Torah
> In the joy of holiness.

God obligates us to be holy not because it is a stretch for us that is aspirational but unachievable. He demands it of us because God believes we can become holy. We, too, must remove our sin and bask in the joy of holiness. It is within our grasp. In the *aggada*, God assured us of the power of change because deep down we may not believe in its possibility. God used the voice of ultimate persuasion because nothing short of the divine would convince us. All is possible. Holiness is within reach.

OPENING THE DOOR FOR *NE'ILA*

Repentance is sometimes the last door that we decide to walk through.

One year, I was at an airport between Rosh HaShana and Yom Kippur, and right near my gate, a man was talking on the phone loudly and gesticulating wildly. "I begged them to keep the door open. I pleaded. You don't understand. They shut the doors. They just wouldn't let me on the flight." Maybe he was talking to his boss or a client. Probably his wife. As he continued to talk, he got more flustered and made more excuses for being late. But the louder he got, the clearer it was that it was his fault. He just wasn't prepared. He got there late, and the doors were already shut.

The doors may be shut, but a door is only a portal. The decision to walk through the door is our own. This transition is magnificently captured by the late poet Adrienne Rich in "Prospective Immigrants Please Note":

> Either you will go through this door
> or you will not go through.

If you go through
there is always the risk
of remembering your name.

Things look at you doubly
and you must look back
and let them happen.

If you do not go through
It is possible
to live worthily

to maintain your attitudes
to hold your position
to die bravely

but much will blind you,
much will evade you,
at what cost who knows?

The door itself makes no promises.
It is only a door.

The gates of heaven are only a door. There is no handbook and no map. There is no promise or guarantee. It is only a door. The door is not a promise, but it is an invitation to launch an adventure and a journey whose destination involves change. We are living in a broken world, and the key to that world is in the door of compassion, *sha'ar haraḥamim*, and the door of repentance, *sha'ar hateshuva*. They remain open even when other doors are closing.

Lamentations Rabba, a collection of midrashim on the book of Lamentations, is the source that tells us that the gates of repentance are always open even if the gates of prayer are about to close (3:44). Some doors shut, others stay open. In Berakhot, we find another talmudic basis for the *Ne'ila* service.

> Rabbi Elazar said: From the day the Temple was destroyed, the heavenly gates of prayer were locked, as it says: "Though I would cry and plead, He shut out my prayer" (Lamentations 3:8). But even though the gates of prayer have been locked, the gates of tears have not been locked, as it is stated, "Hear my prayer, God. Give ear to my cry. To my tears do not be silent" (Psalms 39:13).[10]

We ask not that God see our tears but that God not be silent to our tears. We want God to be engaged in our sorrow, to show compassion when we are desperate, and we stand in front of a door that seems impossible to unlock.

Rabbi Joseph Soloveitchik in his book *Halakhic Man* recalls a moment when he stood with his father in the synagogue courtyard right before *Ne'ila*. It was, in his words, a "fresh, clear day, one of the fine, almost delicate days of summer's end, filled with sunshine and light" that was fast turning into night. His father turned to him and said, "This sunset differs from the ordinary sunsets, for with it forgiveness is bestowed upon us for our sins." As the day changed to night, Rabbi Moses, his father, saw in it the transformation of a soul. At that moment, Rabbi Soloveitchik meditated on what was happening outside with what was happening inside:

> Yom Kippur and the forgiveness of sins merged and blended here with the splendor and beauty of the world and with the hidden lawfulness of the order of creation. The whole was transformed into one living, holy, cosmic phenomenon.[11]

Most of us are in the synagogue as the sun is setting. The fluorescent lighting removes us from the experience of sunset during *Ne'ila*. But if we can look out a window or even step outside for a few minutes before our final prayers begin, we can see the sky carrying the lesson of transformation that we have been trying hard to achieve inside. Everything is turning. Darkness is approaching. The day is ending. We are still alive. We will make it through the fast. We will try again. The possibility of change never leaves us. We think of who we were when we stepped into *Kol Nidrei* and who we are as *Ne'ila* is closing. We are not the same.

We don't have much time left. In a midrash, a *bat kol* (heavenly voice) came down from the sky to tell Moses that he had only three hours left to live. Moses continued to debate God. Let me into the land of Israel. He listed all of his merits. He begged. He pleaded. And then the *bat kol* returned, "Moses, you have only one hour left." And Moses continued to debate God and complain about his fate. And then the *bat kol* came down and said, "Moses, you have only fifteen minutes left."

Squandering the last hours justifying ourselves, we lose the time we thought we had. How are we going to spend the next fifteen minutes? The next half hour? The next hour? The next week? We can beg and plead and make excuses. We can use all of our energy to argue or complain. Or we can use that energy to radiate love, to get a little closer to the people we care about, to bring God into our lives, to make someone else's life a little better. And we can do all this before the gates close.

LIFE HOMEWORK

Exercise 1:

Think of a place or a ritual that is exceptionally holy to you and that brings out your most transcendent self. How can you use it to inspire greater holiness in your life?

Think about the activities you engage in and the time you spend nurturing your physical self through exercise, recreation, or rest. Reduce it to an approximate number of hours a week. Now think about activities or behavior you engage in that have a holy quality. Only include rituals like prayer or study if they contribute to your awareness or experience of holiness, not if they are done as rote or obligatory undertakings. Compare your findings. What did you learn about yourself?

Exercise 2:

Imagine a door that stands in front of you that is getting in the way of your success. Name a problem and visualize it as that door. Stand squarely in front of it. What would it take to open the door? That door is your gate of repentance. It is your *Ne'ila*. Muster the strength to go through it. When you get to the other side, you will realize that it was just a door, a mere threshold into the self. You can cross the threshold.

PASSAGES FOR ADDITIONAL STUDY

Maimonides, *Mishneh Torah, The Laws of Repentance* 10:2–3

> One who serves [God] out of love occupies himself in the Torah and the mitzvot and walks in the paths of wisdom for no ulterior motive: not because of fear that evil will occur, nor in order to acquire benefit. Rather, he does what is true because it is true, and ultimately, good will come because of it. This is a very high level which is not merited by every wise man. It is the level of our patriarch, Abraham, whom God described as, "he who loved Me," for his service was only motivated by love. God commanded us [to seek] this rung [of service] as conveyed by Moses as [Deuteronomy 6:5] states: "Love God, your Lord." When a man will

love God in the proper manner, he will immediately perform all of the mitzvot motivated by love.

What is the proper [degree] of love? That a person should love God with a very great and exceeding love until his soul is bound up in the love of God. Thus, he will always be obsessed with this love as if he is lovesick.

Rabbi Moshe Haim Luzzatto, *The Path of the Just*, "Author's Introduction"

Love of God... if we do not make an effort to implant it in our hearts, utilizing all of the means which direct us towards it, how will it exist within us? When will it enter into our soul's intimacy and ardor towards the Blessed One and towards His Torah if we do not give heart to His greatness and majesty which engender this intimacy in our hearts?

Rabbi Abraham Isaac Kook, *The Lights of Repentance* 13:11

Great and sublime is the happiness of repentance. The consuming fire of sin's pain in itself refines, resulting in a superior and radiant purification of character, till the great wealth of repentance to be found in the treasure of life develops and unfolds before him. Humans continue to ascend through repentance, through its bitterness and its pleasantness, through its sorrow and its joy; nothing refines and purifies man, truly uplifting him to the level of man, as does the profound contemplation of repentance, "In the place where the penitents stand even the wholly righteous cannot stand" (Berakhot 34a).

Text questions to think about while studying:

- Why is repentance from love superior to repentance from fear?
- What is the connection between holiness and teshuva?
- How can we achieve greater intimacy with God through teshuva?

Notes

1. Rudolph Otto, *The Idea of the Holy* (Oxford: Oxford University Press, 1958).
2. Numbers Rabba 12:4, as translated by Lawrence Kushner in *Eyes Remade for Wonder* (Woodstock, VT: Jewish Lights, 1998), 17.
3. Kushner, *Eyes Remade for Wonder*, 18.
4. Milton Steinberg, *As a Driven Leaf* (Springfield, NJ: Behrman House, 1996).
5. *Yalkut Shimoni*, Psalm 25.
6. Rabbi Joseph Soloveitchik, *On Repentance* (Jerusalem: Oroth Publishing House, 1980), 273.
7. Martin Buber, *Tales of the Hasidim: Later Masters* (New York: Schocken Books, 1977), 253.
8. Pesaḥim 54a.
9. John Kotter, *The Heart of Change* (Boston: Harvard Business School Press, 2002), 1.
10. Berakhot 32b.
11. Rabbi Joseph Soloveitchik, *Halakhic Man* (Philadelphia: Jewish Publication Society, 1984), 38.

Epilogue

The Day After

In the last chapter of the talmudic tractate Yoma, our sages of old debated the merits of repentance and its limitations. What can teshuva change and what can it not change? In one particularly moving passage, different rabbis put forward noble statements about why teshuva is an incredible gift, usually based on a close reading of a biblical verse.

Rabbi Hama bar Hanina began the great debate, held in Socratic style. "Great is repentance," he believed, "for it brings healing to the world, as it is said: 'I will heal their backsliding. I will love them freely' (Hosea 14:5)." Through the act of teshuva, God is able to hold us up to our own best standard. When we find ourselves sliding back into a place we never wanted to go, we remind ourselves that we can change and that the change will bring inner healing to ourselves and the world. God loves us freely and unconditionally, but it is harder to feel that love when there is too much distance. *Close the gap.*

Rabbi Levi observed: "Great is repentance, for it reaches up to the Throne of Glory, as it is said: 'Return O Israel, unto the Lord, your God, for you have stumbled in your sin' (Hosea 14:2)." Rabbi Levi took the verse literally. We return to the Lord. When we return, we create access to God. The remoteness that results from sin is abolished, leaving only intimacy with God. *Reach higher.*

Resh Lakish said, "Great is repentance, for because of it premeditated sins are accounted as mere errors, as it is said: 'Return O Israel, unto the Lord, your God, for you have stumbled in your sin.'" Resh Lakish took the same verse as his esteemed colleague but interpreted the latter part rather than the former. Sinning is an act of stumbling. When we try to make up for the faltering path that sin leads us down, our sins are mistakes rather than intentional acts of self-destruction. *Pick yourself up.*

Rabbi Samuel bar Nahmani said in the name of Rabbi Jonathan: "Great is repentance, because it prolongs the years of a person, as it is said: 'And when the wicked turns from his wickedness…he shall live' (Ezekiel 33:19)." Teshuva is an elixir of life. When people commit to change, they give themselves a new life and find possibilities that they formerly believed were closed to them. *Open the door.*

Rabbi Meir used to say: "Great is repentance, since even if only one person repents, the sins of the world are forgiven, as it is said: 'I will heal their backsliding, I will love them freely for My anger is turned away from him' (Hosea 14:5)." Rabbi Meir read this verse carefully and noticed the odd change from the third person plural to the third person singular. "Their" is replaced in the end by "him." Rabbi Meir understood that this implied that God forgives the entire nation when even one person does teshuva. As preposterous as it sounds, Rabbi Kook turned this passage's meaning on its head in *The Lights of Repentance*. God, he believed, would not forgive an entire universe if only one person changed his decadent or immoral ways. Rather, Rabbi Kook read this passage very personally: if one person repents then the whole world changes in his eyes. It is not that the world improves; it is that the person who changes adopts a new attitude and perspective. Objects of scorn and derision become less abhorrent. People and places associated with negativity take on a more positive spin. When we change, the world looks different to us. *Look at the world anew.*

If we close our eyes, we can almost imagine a study hall brimming with inspiring debate. No one is exclusively right in this debate, but no one is wrong either. The merits of any mitzva are subjective to the performer of that commandment. Each sage quoted in the Talmud felt an affinity for the mandate to repent, and each saw in the act of repentance a distinct advantage. The layering of each answer has a multiplier effect, helping us appreciate in all of its various ways the positive impact of authentic change.

As you look back on the past ten days, you may find yourself at the center of this ancient conversation. As each day progressed, you may have distilled your experience through Rabbi Hama bar Hanina's lens. Teshuva is healing. You may have interpreted the verse in Hosea like Rabbi Levi; repentance helped you return to God or to a self you liked better than the self you were before the season began. Resh Lakish may have helped you look back on your own transgressions with mercy and compassion, helping you move them from intention to regrettable mistakes that can be repaired. You may feel more alive and thank Rabbi Samuel bar Nahmani for his insight. You may engage in silent dialogue with Rabbi Meir and consider the ways that the world surrounding you has changed in these past ten days, not because it has changed but because you have.

Conversations like this one invite us into their pages. Stepping in, I invite you to write your own conclusion to this talmudic argument.

"Great is repentance, because..."

When you finish the sentence in your own words, you will be able to see just how much teshuva as an act of return takes place every day, not merely on one day or in one month or over a few holidays. We return and then we return again. We have to keep returning because we change, and the world around us changes. In a universe without stasis, we cannot be caught standing still. The majestic endeavor of discovering human purpose beckons each and every day. And every day, we are invited to respond to that call. *Hineni.* I am here and fully present.

Return.

About the Author

Dr. Erica Brown is a writer and educator who lectures widely on subjects of Jewish interest. She is scholar-in-residence for the Jewish Federation of Greater Washington, DC, and a consultant to other Jewish organizations. Dr. Brown is the author of *Confronting Scandal, Spiritual Boredom, Inspired Jewish Leadership,* and *In the Narrow Places: Daily Inspiration for the Three Weeks,* and is co-author of *The Case for Jewish Peoplehood.* She lives with her husband and four children in Silver Spring, MD.

For more information about Dr. Brown's work, visit www.leadingwithmeaning.com.

The fonts used in this book are from the Arno family

Other works by Erica Brown
available from Maggid Books:

In the Narrow Places:
Daily Inspiration for the Three Weeks

Maggid Books
The best of contemporary Jewish thought from
Koren Publishers Jerusalem